The Sewing Connection

Shirley Adams

Series 17

The Sewing Connection Series 17

1 *Coming Up Roses* 3
Celebrate a fuchsia boiled wool jacket with couched knotted yarns, buttons, beads, set-in sleeves, and a silky lining.

2 *Royal Princess Lines* 7
Create the perfect fit for shapely and elegant lines with seams and darts.

3 *Color Me Clever* 12
Create an origami top with six squares of fabric, cut, folded, and joined into a bias. Patternless with hand-woven fiber and suede finished edges.

4 *Gray Skies* 17
Turn gray fabric bright with a parade of kimono-silk umbrellas on a vest, fun kimono sachet.

5 *Water Colors* 21
Quilted layers of sheer fabric create firmness for vests or jackets; triple sheer handkerchief skirt, sheer ocean blue vest with complimentary beading.

6 *Deep Purple* 25
Microfiber leather in eggplant is the basis of a stunning and decoratively quilted vest and jacket. Set in those sleeves without puckers.

7 *Paint the Town Red* 29
Racy faux leather driving jacket with brilliant crystal zippers.

8 *Color Blocking* 38
Create new fresh fabric by combining leftovers and odds. Color coordinate thread, edging, linings for similarity of care and style. One garment will coordinate many garments.

9 *Collecting Color* 42
Assemble fabric, notions, accessories into color groups. Fish leather- Barramundi - becomes a shoulder bag, scraps bloom into a garden on a denim jacket.

10 *Wildly Colorful* 47
Tame wild oversize panel prints, create lovely garments by reconsidering pattern placement.

11 *Changing Colors* 51
A hand-woven purple jacket creates wardrobe combinations by weaving into it extra yarns.

12 *Neutral Accents* 55
Fabrics distinctive yet subtle in color lend texture and design to other fabrics.

13 *Coat of Many Colors* 60
Create a colorful jacket of hand-woven silk that builds an elegant wardrobe of styles. Pattern layout, fabric care, seams, edging, fasteners, and pockets. Make a belted blouse in royal blue.

Shirley and her husband, John, launched *The Sewing Connection* a simple plan and their life savings. The Sewing Connection Seventeen originally aired on public television throughout the United States and beyond. Shirley offers sensible and professional techniques and inspiration to beginners and experts alike.

By utilizing the help of family and friends, *The Sewing Connection* became the standard of fashion design and sewing instruction upon which the industry was built. Shirley designs for sewers who enjoy the art and demand quality that is almost unobtainable in ready-to-wear. The American Sewing Guild continues the guidance and professionalism.

• ISBN 1-884389-37-5 • Sewing Connection •
• www.sewingconnection.com
• Original Copyright © 1997
• SC017.v2 Second Printing 2002
• SC017.v3 Digital Publishing 2010
• SC017.v9 Digital Publishing 2019

Coming Up Roses

Chapter 1

Welcome to The Sewing Connection Series Seventeen. As you look through the offerings in a fabric store you want to touch, squeeze, drape each piece of fabric. The tactile quality is irresistible but what initially attracts you? Probably the color! Everyone has favorite colors and that's going to be the theme of this whole series as we concentrate first on one, then another. When I look at the wonderful colors and start working with fabrics I always feel everything's coming up roses!

I hear from so many viewers "I really don't need any more clothes – but I just love to sew". That says to me you want only to do the fun things, the pretty things, and so do I. We're therefore going to do a lot of embellishing, a lot of fabric mixing, a lot of art-to-wear because this is all definitely classified as fun.

It's a good idea to periodically shop the expensive ready-to-wear just to be sure you're on target with your sewing plans. I recently took a day to browse and was pleased to see so much in the embellishment and mixing categories. Fashion really has a light-hearted "up" mood right now and that's certainly in line with my personal feeling and thinking. It's a pleasure to explore such happy clothing before going to shop the fabric stores. This gives you a chance to firm up preferences and ideas, gives an insight into the direction fashion is heading and answers questions you might have about handling a particular fabric. Also some find it difficult to decide what would be personally flattering as you look through pattern books. In the ready-to-wear there's no question. Try on different things to see what looks best before selecting similar patterns and fabrics and colors.

Boiled wool has always been a classic seen especially in fitted Austrian jackets. This year its appearing in every price range and in a larger variety of styles. I was really happy to see this as I had just bought a piece and am so glad the timing is right!

Boiled wool hadn't actually interested me very much until I spotted a piece in a rosy warm rhubarb color (which you see on the cover) and I was hooked. Color is indeed the grabber.

Boiled wool begins as a sweater knit - then purposely goes awry. It is washed in hot water, rinsed in cold, dried in a hot dryer. It comes out "fulled" or shrunken to a smaller size and thicker, denser than the original piece. It still retains some of the knit stretch unless you choose to line it as I did. This stabilizes it, but the usual way is to leave it unlined. When "boiled" in this way we usually see the wrong side, the purl stitch, becomes the right side of the garment.

Traditionally these jackets have had princess seams, making it easy to shape those curvy lines to your figure. As a designer-sewer the choice is always yours. I chose very simple side seams, only in a boxy jacket, nothing elaborate. The embellishment on the jacket would be its highlight, so don't clutter it up with any extra seams. If your pattern has side darts, this extra fabric could be merely eased in to fit, providing some curves. That excess is then steam pressed flat but the fullness is still there for comfort.

Let's consider seaming possibilities. When you cut it out the raw edges are in no danger of falling apart or raveling out. The fulling process makes everything quite secure. The seam choice may depend on how thick the fabric is. If still relatively light weight, regular seams may be stitched, then pressed open. Another option is to topstitch on each side of the stitching line if that look pleases you. Or trim one allowance short and press the longer seam over it for a flat-felled seam look. This would then be topstitched to hold in place. Either of these could have some decorative stitch if you like that effect. If there is too much give or stretch in the shoulder seam, tape it to stabilize. This could be a fusible tape, a narrow sew-in twill tape, a rayon seam tape, or even the trimmed - off narrow selvage of a lining fabric if it will be concealed and not show on the jacket inside. Typically there will be a shoulder pad (lining covering or not) to preserve its shape. If no lining, cover the pad with a lining fabric of matching color. Even if seams are stabilized remember there will still be plenty of give in the fabric interiors. Don't make this jacket too big, allowing for this eventuality.

In The Sewing Connection series 15 there were some marvelous jackets borrowed from people who had recycled wool sweaters to piece together after shrinking the fabric. These were too heavy for regular seaming. One choice there is to butt together the raw edges and connect with a decorative machine stitch. You probably have on your machine several appropriate choices that would work. Another is to zigzag the edges together, then cover the joining with a strip of

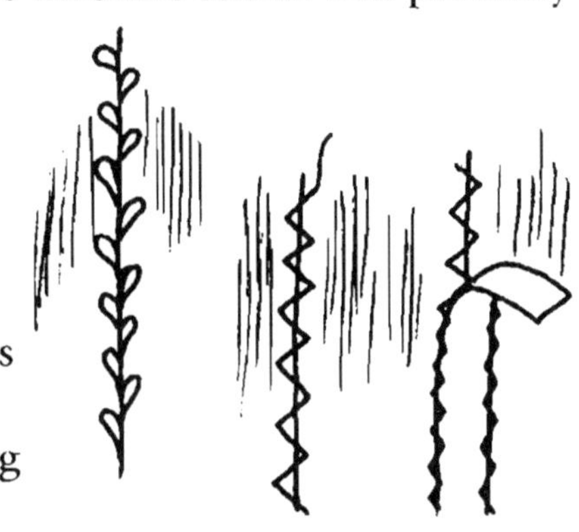

another fabric. Good choices would be wool jersey, synthetic suede or leather. Any of these would be cut about $1/2$" wide on the cross grain of the fabric to allow for some stretch to shape around curves if any exist.

Although serger finishing the cut edges is unnecessary to prevent raveling, you might choose to flatlock a seam using decorative thread in the upper looper. This is then opened flat and it is like a hinge rather than a bulky seam. The thread used can be woolly nylon, Luny (wool thread), rayon ribbon floss, heavy embroidery or pearl rayon, or metallic.

Ordinarily interfacing would be in the process after cutting out the fabric and before constructing the garment. Typically, no

interfacing is used in boiled wool so it just doesn't enter into this picture. With the usual boiled wool techniques partially accounted for, let me tell you what paths I took.

For starters is cutting out. My machine knit was in a tubular piece so the first test is checking with a steam iron to see if the side creases will press out. If a trace of them remains, refold the piece so the creases fall between pattern pieces, or at least in some unobtrusive place. Rub your hand lightly in both directions to see if there is a discernible nap. If yes, lay all pattern pieces with the nap in the down direction. If not, save space by putting pieces down in both directions. Typically no facings are used so you gain some space in their absence. I was only using a one-piece back, the two fronts and two sleeves. With only $1\frac{1}{2}$ yards of slightly narrow fabric, they wouldn't fit, lacking about **4"** in width.

Coming up a little short of fabric is not a worry. A combination of fabrics is very interesting and gives you a creative challenge. On the double thickness' of fabric I decided to supplement a stripe down the center of each sleeve. Usually it's on the body of a jacket, towards the center or up around the neck where most attention is drawn with embellishment or contrast trims. Just for something completely different, mine would be in the center of each sleeve.

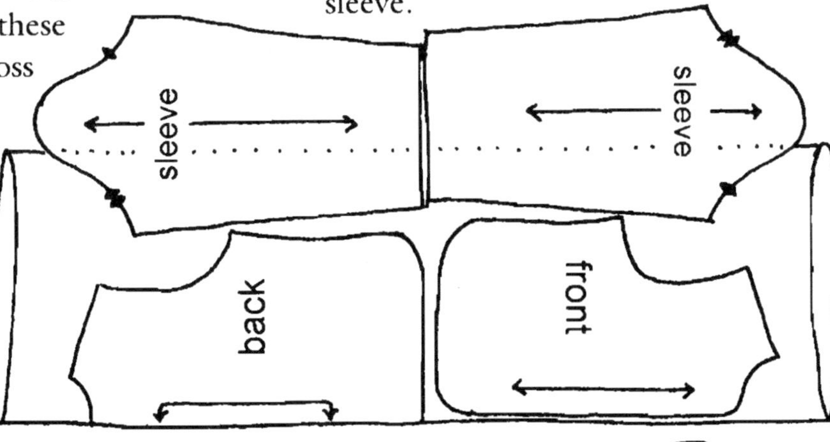

A trip to a wonderful local fabric shop produced a lightweight wool crepe in the same color, but in a slightly brighter intensity. It would work very well as the two-piece dress under the jacket and the supplementary fabric in the sleeve

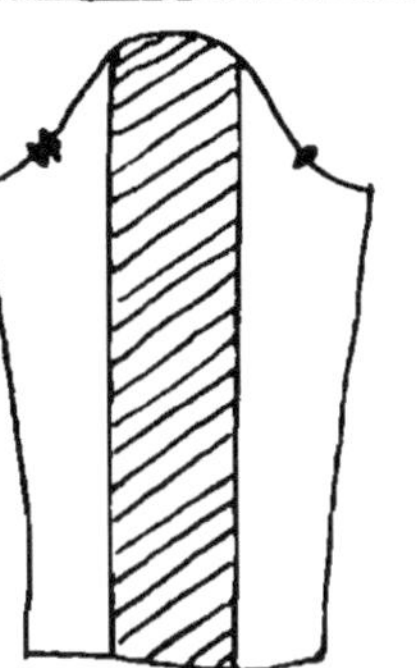

center. Only one problem in the sleeve insert it looked too bright. Solution: embellish to partially obscure the brightness. This is the fun of sewing. This is why I don't have a staff of people sewing the garments I demonstrate. I love to come up with exactly *what* solution will do the job.

I don't have the answers in advance. Instead I look around in all the drawers in my sewing room heavily laden with treasures collected from everywhere I travel. My "resource center" is an accumulation of anything interesting I see in any shop. I know someday it will be exactly what I need so I buy it even though, at the moment, its ultimate destination is an unknown. Don't you just love the excitement of sewing! Like reading a mystery novel, you never exactly know the outcome until the last page.

What resources I accumulated were an assortment of clay and stone beads, rugged rather than glitzy, complementary to the honest earthy fabrics. They come from Australia, San Diego, Santa Fe and were all in deep red tones blending with the fabric color. In my yarn drawer was a ball of wool variegated from reds, burgundies, deep pinks into an occasional olive segment. This is the biggest pleasure, the most fun of sewing – assembling everything that belongs.

The embellishment on those crepe sleeve insets began with several rows of twin needle pintucks down the center. The addition of some texture was fun, but not the finish. It was joined by many rows of the variegated yarns couched at regular intervals either side of the pintucks. Couching is zigzag stitching over the yarn, possibly with monofilament (invisible) nylon thread on top, any thread in the bobbin. Try any of a number of presser feet to hold the yarn in place as you stitch over it. This time, because the pintuck foot was already on the machine, I found it worked perfectly, holding the yarn in one of the grooves. Sewing with the needle down position, it held the yarn and fabric

in place every time I stopped to tie a knot for added textural interest. Then stitching over the loosely tied knots followed. Those sleeves were getting busier by the minute but my favorite part was sewing on all the beads by hand here and there as it felt appropriate. These were a variety of shapes ... flat doughnuts, cylinders, cubes. On television there were a few of these added. Now a few months later, an additional multitude joined the melange as evidenced on the book's cover.

After constructing the jacket and sewing pads in the shoulder area, I decided to add a lining before binding the edges. This felt more complete and, since it would be worn over a wool dress, would slip on and off easily. Stretch in the final product was not a concern, so I cut that lining on the straight. A center back pleat allows for comfortable reaching without straining the lining fabric. If you want a lining that stretches everywhere, you could either use a knit tricot or cut the woven lining on the bias.

Typically for the edge finish, purchased fold-over braid is used. Sometimes you can find some made by the same knitter to match your fabric. If not, consider other alternatives. Fold-over suede might be another choice. To press a strip of suede in half accurately is difficult with a press cloth on top since visibility is obscured. Don't press-sew. Fold the strip *not quite* in half, the underside a little longer. Edge stitch close to the fold and it will be done perfectly, readjusting as needed. This foldover is sandwiched over the raw edge(s) of the jacket and lining which have been staystitched together. Stitch the suede open edges and it connects everything making a lovely finish. The front side will have the edgestitching on each edge. The backside will have a longer edge beyond the stitching in order to catch everything. Trim off extra if you prefer.

Synthetic leather can be used to bind (cut on the crosswise for greater stretch), but in a two-step method. Right sides together, stitch the trim to the jacket edge with a $\frac{1}{4}$" seam. Flip the trim to the backside covering the original stitching line. From the front side stitch in the ditch and it isn't noticeable. The backside will have excess leather beyond the stitching line that you can trim if you prefer.

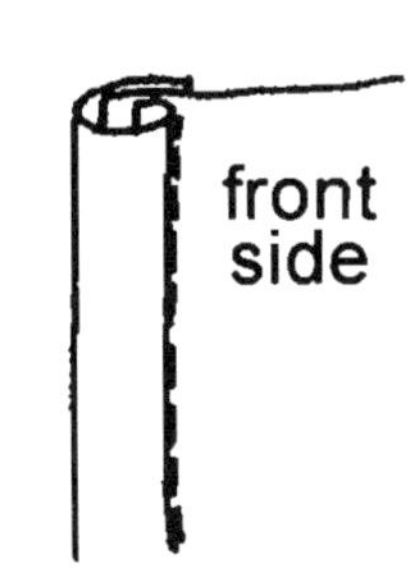

The same thing can be done with fabric, the strips bias cut if woven, crosswise if knit. The only difference is the strip width. Cut a little wider in fabric so the back edge can be turned under for a finished edge. To keep this edging soft you might opt to hand stitch the backside down rather than machine stitching in the ditch.

For a little variation in that trim, mine is striped with more of the yarn couched down in straight rows on the straight grain of the fabric. The rows are irregularly spaced for added interest. Before couching the fabric was cut at a 45° angle, top and bottom. After couching, lines were drawn at regular intervals with a ruler. The width of the bias strips that will result I chose to be $1\frac{3}{4}$".

Pin the two straight sides together, offsetting them one strip width. On the above sketch, the two **X**s would be matched up. Stitch a narrow seam so the fabric is now in a cylinder. This seam will spiral around the cylinder parallel to the couched yarn stripes. Begin cutting at the scissors and it will cut round and round so you end up with one long continuous bias strip.

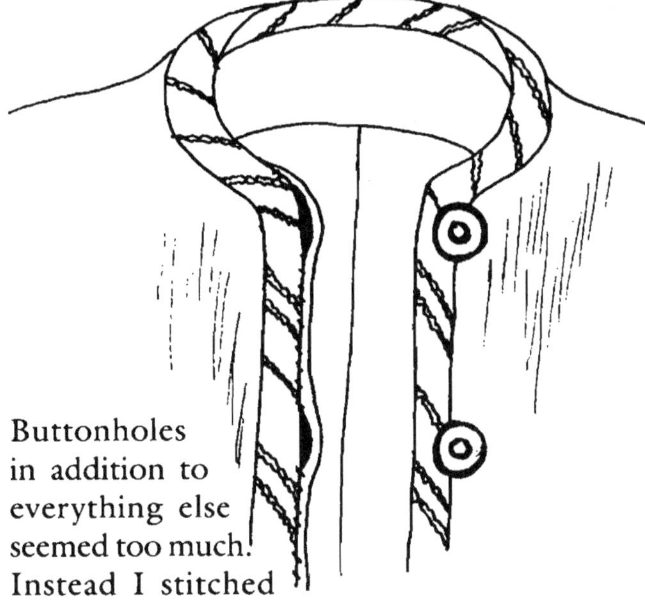

Buttonholes in addition to everything else seemed too much! Instead I stitched and turned a narrow tube of the plain woven wool, and added it to the jacket right front edge. I stitched this on with invisible hand stitches, leaving an open space each place a button loop was needed to match up with the buttons.

The buttons seen on television were yarn ball buttons. Make by placing a 6" strand of yarn parallel to a pencil. With a separate strand of yarn (do not cut off yet), wind around the original yarn and pencil about 30 to 50 times, whatever it takes to make the size ball you want. Take the two original yarn ends and tie in a knot. Carefully slide the whole mass off the pencil and tighten the knot to secure. Trim off ends and stitch securely to the garment for a button. You can see on the book cover, I later replaced these with commercial buttons.

The jacket has patch pockets, yarns couched on the top edge. Set the machine on a narrow zigzag and stitch on and off the pocket. The stitches bury themselves in the texture and do not show.

Create a little magic in everything you sew making it an original unlike any other.

Royal Princess Lines *Chapter 2*

These past several months I've become increasingly aware of more fitted fashions than we've seen for a long time. You have only to look through shops and catalogs to see curved princess seams everywhere. This is quite a change from the shapeless oversize garments popular for so long. When woven fabrics are fitted they have to incorporate shape. This can be in the form of darts or curved seams and actually, it takes some of the former to turn into the latter.

There are princess-lined patterns of course, but if you use any of these commercial patterns you may want to rethink your size. It is possible that you'll have to go a size larger than you're used to buying.

If you make your own patterns from a basic, either a paper commercial pattern or a Bonfit adjustable pattern, you will need to add some ease. Any basic fitting pattern does just that – fits. There is enough room to breathe and move in it, but clothing is worn a little larger than this basic. I always build into the bodice about 2" more than what is provided.

Measure your bust plus the desired ease and compare this number with the measured pattern pieces. This tells you how much room you need to add. Let's begin with darts manipulated in series 16 and go on from there.

It is imperative that these darts point right to your bust. The look is unflattering if dart points are higher or lower than your bust apex. Raise or lower the original darts so they are in exactly the correct place. It then follows that the princess lines developed from the darted bodice will also have the curve at the right level.

If you are using a princess pattern and (for example), the bust point needs to be moved down **1"**, slash the pattern above its apex. Separate the top and bottom as necessary and insert, then tape the connecting paper. Restore the proper length by folding out an equal amount of paper below the bust. Smooth out any jagged outer lines (called truing).

Whether you start with a Bonfit adjustable pattern, commercial paper patterns, or finished fashion patterns, fine-tuning for a precise fit will always be necessary.

The most common dart combination is an underarm and a waist dart. Manipulate this up to the shoulder by slashing a new line down to the bust from mid-shoulder. Tape together the side dart, and the shoulder automatically opens up. This combination of darts is the common location for princess lines. Hash mark above and below the bust as shown. These little marks become notches to match together the finished pattern once it is split into two pieces.

Now go ahead and pull apart the two pieces joined only at the bust point. Add seam allowances to each and turn the hash marks into notches. You now have a complete bodice front princess line as easily as that! Add grain arrows so you know how to lay it on the fabric. In this case, the center front is to be cut on the fold as seen by the curved arrow ends. The side

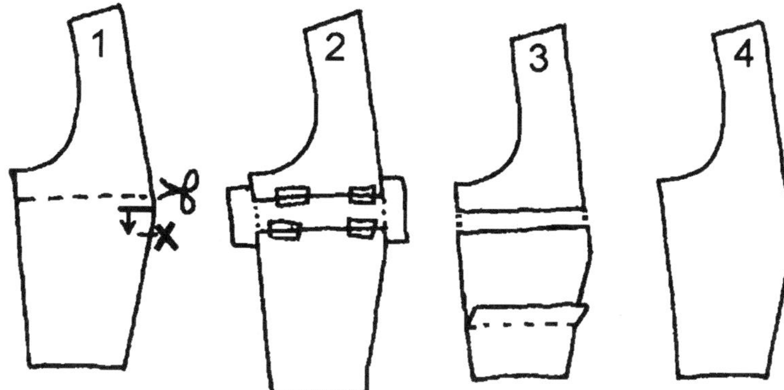

front panel is divided approximately in half to determine where the grain arrows will be. The finished bodice front would look like this.

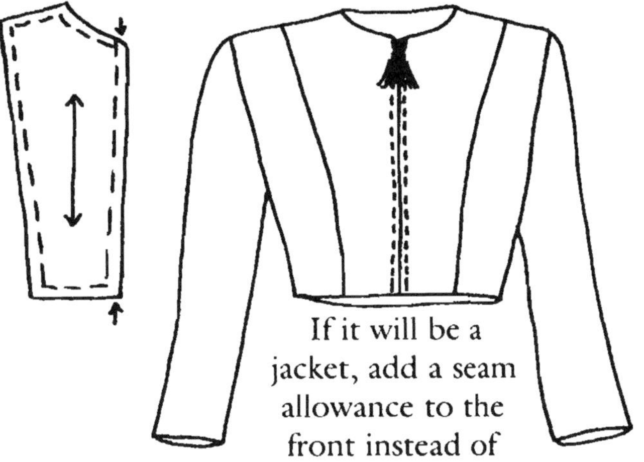

If it will be a jacket, add a seam allowance to the front instead of cutting it on the fold and you could have a zipper closing – very popular now.

Add an extension for buttons and buttonholes and a shaped lapel and it will look like this. Once you realize what these simple changes can do and how easy it is to do them, there is no end to your creativity!

The two-piece dress I wore under the jacket in program **1** had an extended bodice to cover the upper hip area – worn as an over top. Do this by using a skirt pattern with a simple basic dart and adding the side to the bodice side. The center front skirt is added to the bodice center front overlapping the waistline at the $^5/_8$" stitching line. To break the hip line it might be more flattering to curve it instead of using a

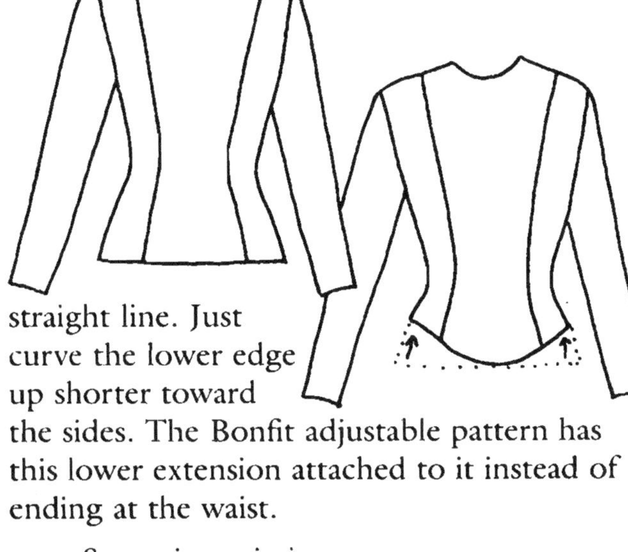

straight line. Just curve the lower edge up shorter toward the sides. The Bonfit adjustable pattern has this lower extension attached to it instead of ending at the waist.

Sometimes in overtops or suit jackets that lower line is broken by leaving the lower few inches of the princess seam open. It would then be finished by a wider hem or facing, or even by hand stitching finished lining edges to it.

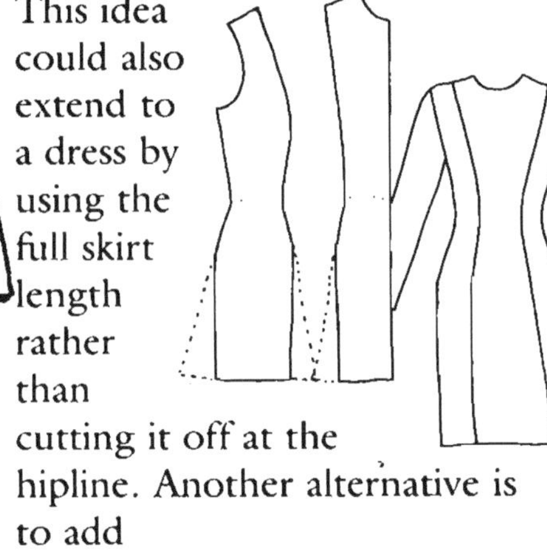

This idea could also extend to a dress by using the full skirt length rather than cutting it off at the hipline. Another alternative is to add flare to each seam in the skirt and have a flared skirt on the dress rather than a straight one. If you found all this easy, let's move on to other possibilities.

Cut a slash in the armscye and tape the underarm dart closed. You end up with another popular look.

Usually princess lines intersect the bust point, but sometimes they're located slightly to the side. In this event there will also **need to be a small dart** or the easing in of excess fabric.

Just like darts can be moved to any location as long as they point to the bust, so can princess lines or curved seams. Typically they are more vertical as those already done, but they can go in other directions as well. Also unlike

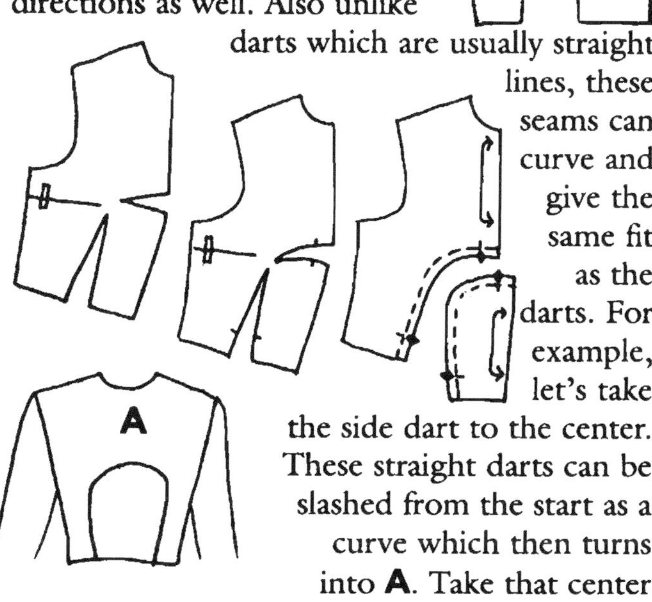

darts which are usually straight lines, these seams can curve and give the same fit as the darts. For example, let's take the side dart to the center. These straight darts can be slashed from the start as a curve which then turns into **A**. Take that center line, eliminate the waist dart and slash from the armscye to make a fitted yoke line. Of course, curve the center line upward for a fluid line – or not.

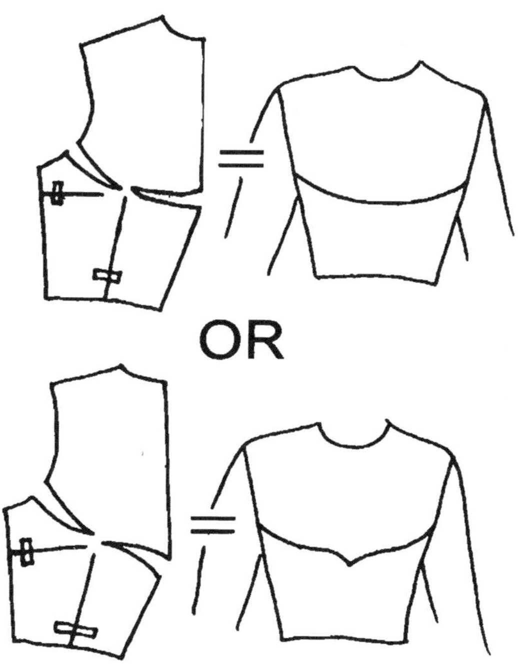

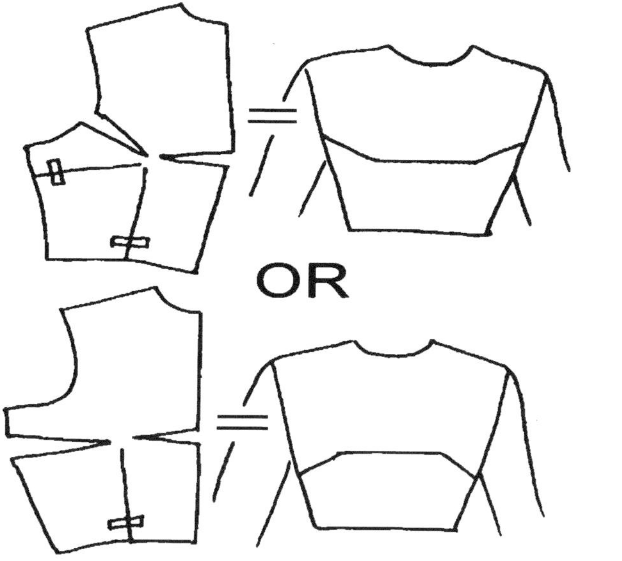

Maybe these variations are done on plain fabric accented by topstitching, or piping

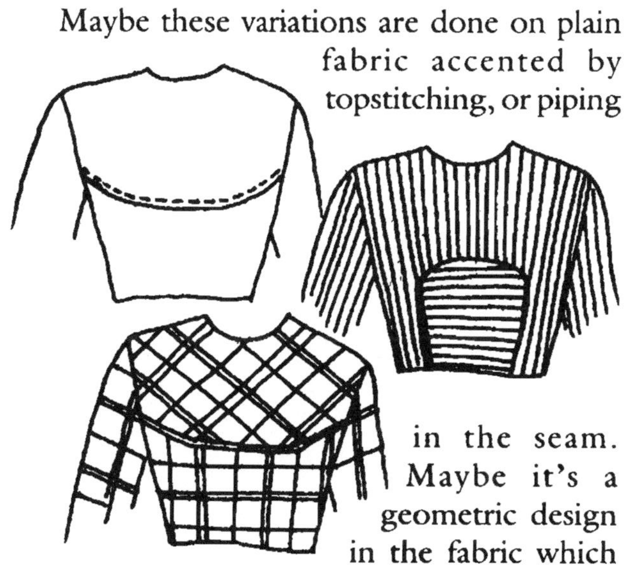

in the seam. Maybe it's a geometric design in the fabric which provides impact, or color blocks.

Any of these variations are best done first in miniature to judge the optical illusion created. Some changes can make a bust look larger or smaller. Some will broaden or **narrow shoulders** or waist. Determine which are most flattering before doing them in full size and being surprised at the results.

The slant or curve of the vertical choices make a difference in your visual body proportions. If they curve in or out on top, the shoulder width is affected.

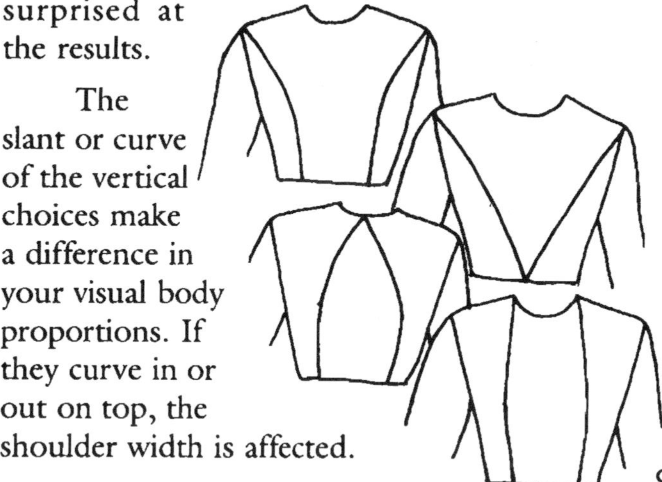

If you feel adventurous, fullness can be added in princess lines. Consider a formal or party dress, for example. The bodice sides may be all gathered by slashing and spreading it open to perhaps twice or more its original length in the paper pattern. Cut out the fabric and gather it up to the finished size usually using a plain lining underneath to preserve the size.

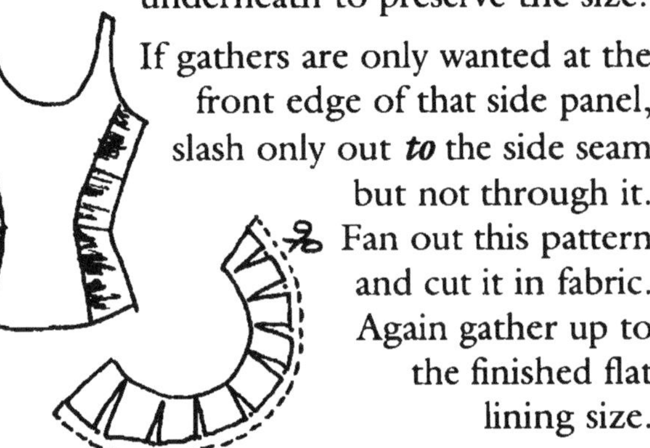

If gathers are only wanted at the front edge of that side panel, slash only out *to* the side seam but not through it. Fan out this pattern and cut it in fabric. Again gather up to the finished flat lining size.

These could also have been pleats instead of gathers or the fullness could all be in the center panel, the sides left plain and flat for stabilizing. The possibilities are limitless.

Consider some asymmetrical lines. This will take a *whole* pattern front rather than the usual one half, since both sides are different. This is produced by four completely different darts but notice that both lines intersect the bust apex so it produces a fit. All original darts are taped together after slashing the new ones. Hash

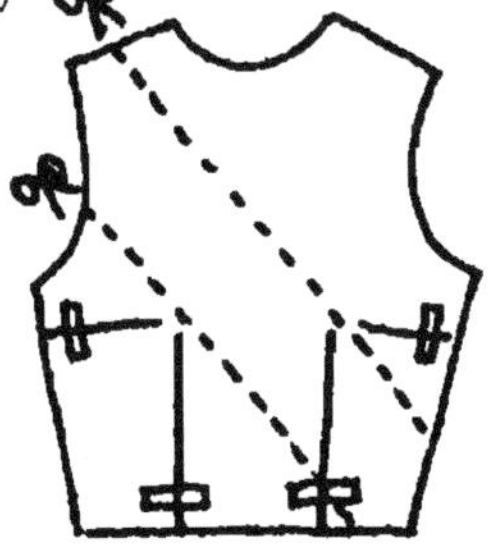

mark the new ones as usual. Pull apart the connections at the bust and the bodice is in three pieces. Add seams and notches and your pattern is complete. The grain arrows may stay on the straight or you can cut it all on the bias if you so choose.

Even though you start out making a complete pattern for the security and comprehension it reinforces, you soon take shortcuts when you thoroughly understand what's happening. I would now cut the pattern apart and lay it on the fabric without completing seams, etc. They can be chalk-marked on the fabric after pinning the pattern in place. I usually just put pins perpendicular to the cutting line extending outward to remind myself to add the seams. Any of this pattern work is very fast once you understand what is needed and how to get there.

These were but a few ideas for princess seams on the bodice front. Invent some combinations of your own for interesting results. The bodice back usually has princess lines as well, to go along with the front. There are always exceptions, however, and you may prefer to leave darts in back.

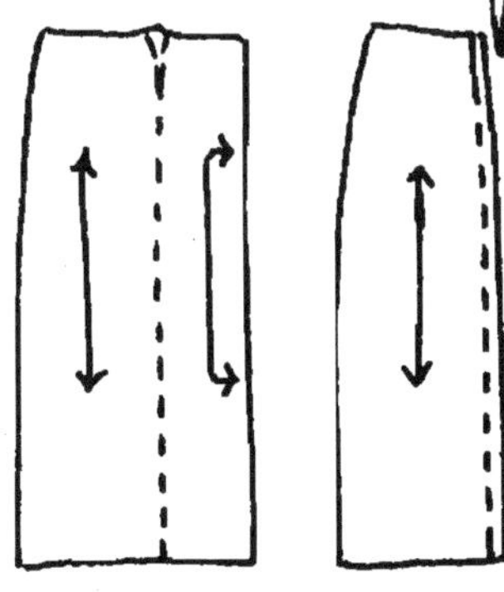

A skirt shown on this same program began as a standard basic straight skirt with darts front and back. To make it a gored skirt, simply cut apart at the dart on down to the hem. The dart is discarded after being cut out and seams are added to each cut edge. When sewn together it has the same shape and fits the same as when it was darted.

My skirt was also lengthened to lower calf length and flared at each gore line. Think at what level this flare would have to be added for maximum comfort and wearability. If added only

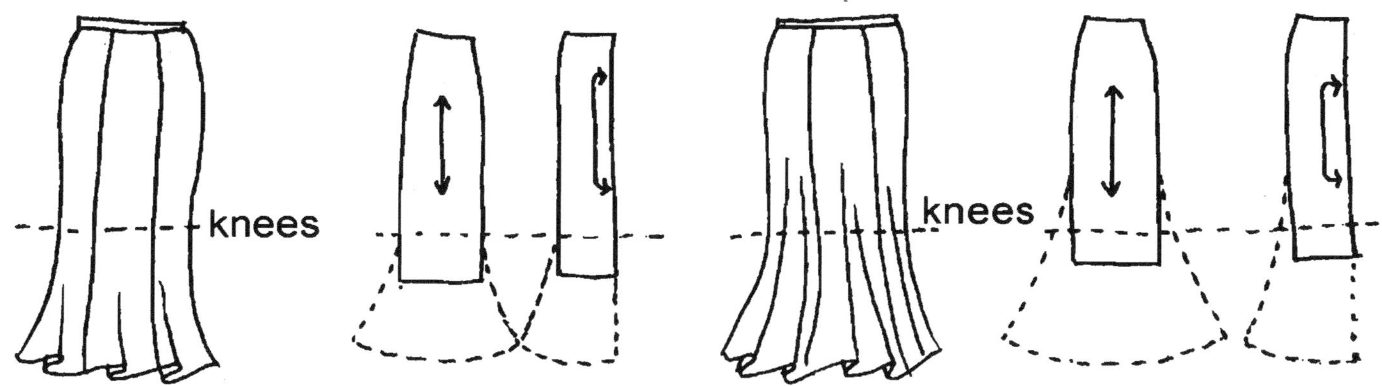

below the knee like this, your walking stride would be restricted. Think instead how much knee room you need (reason for slits, vents, kick pleats in a straight skirt) and begin flaring above the knee accordingly.

Don't you just love the freedom of designing anything you find personally appealing and flattering! All this is within your capabilities regardless of your experience level. Sewing is all common sense developing an understanding of how things work.

Shirley has used permanent patterns in the past, but you may fuse a medium to heavy weight iron-on fusible backing to your pattern and it will last for a very long time, or you can make your own with adjustable sizing using cardboard, glue, brass rivets or Round-Head Fasteners from an office supply store.

www.instructables.com/id/Turn-a-Commercial-Pattern-into-a-Permanent-Pattern,

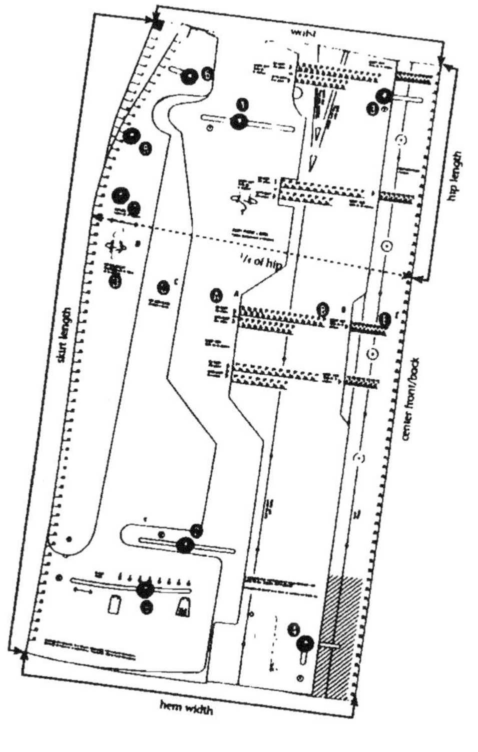

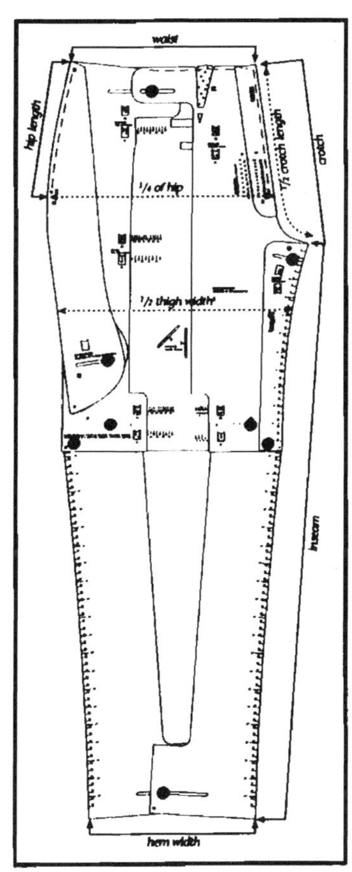

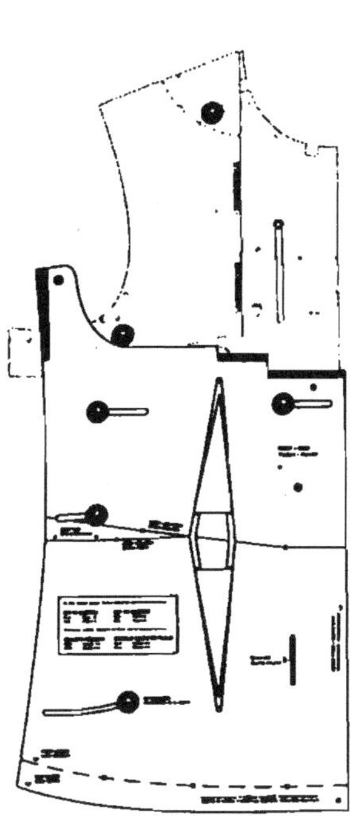

Color Me Clever
Origami Top

We've just added many architectural lines to garments by cutting and seaming. There are still other ways to make flat fabric into rounded body shapes. As a child, did you fold papers this way and that to create an animal or an airplane or something else surprising? Fabric can also be folded in unusual ways to produce unbelievable garments. How about tilting it on the bias, folding it here and there until it becomes wearable!

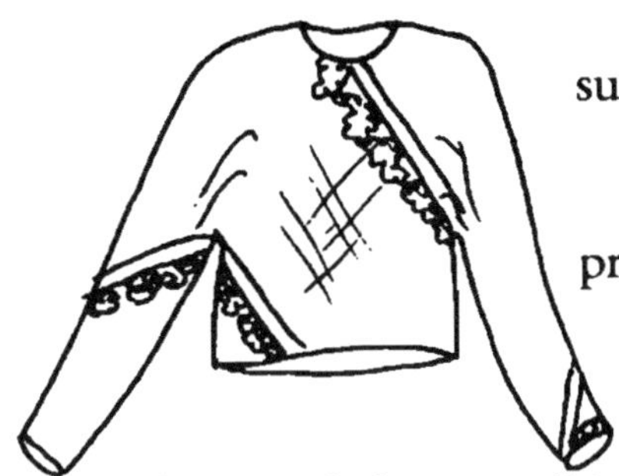

This wasn't my original idea. A sewing friend in Texas, Judy Rand, told me about this and the concept actually came over from Japan. It all hangs on the bias for a flattering fit and once you catch on, the simplicity is amazing!

It involves six squares. Their sizes determine completed garment size. You wouldn't necessarily want the same size. In a heavier fabric you might want this to be more fitted. While a very thin fabric might demand a larger garment to avoid looking skimpy.

If it will be opened down the front to make a jacket, it needs to be larger. It is the same with a casual top. If this will be a dressy garment, it might be more closely fitted. Consider the fabric qualities and the garments intended use to make this decision. Since every bit of this garment will be on the bias, remember this will also effect the fit, making it stretch out a bit longer and narrower. The softer and looser the weave, the more lengthwise stretch.

Let's give this a quick run through just so you understand the concept first. Then we'll get down to more detailed instructions.

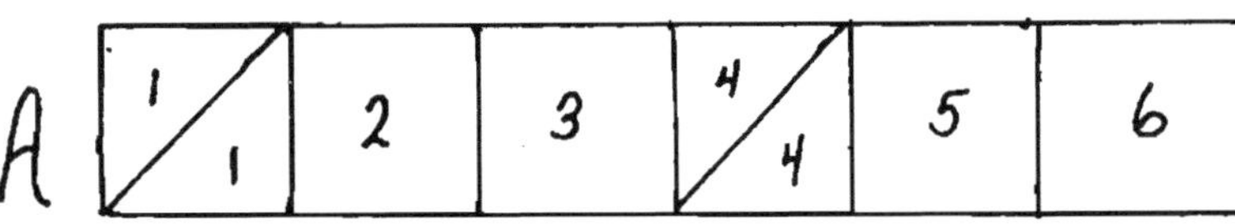

We'll begin with a length of fabric that is six squares all connected, diagonally marked through #1 and #4.

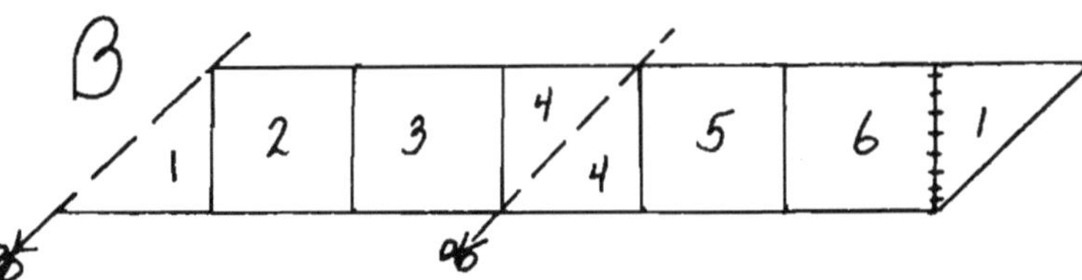

Cut on the diagonal of #1 and sew it on the end of #6. Also cut the diagonal of #4. Now line up the two strips, one on top of the other, and stitch together.

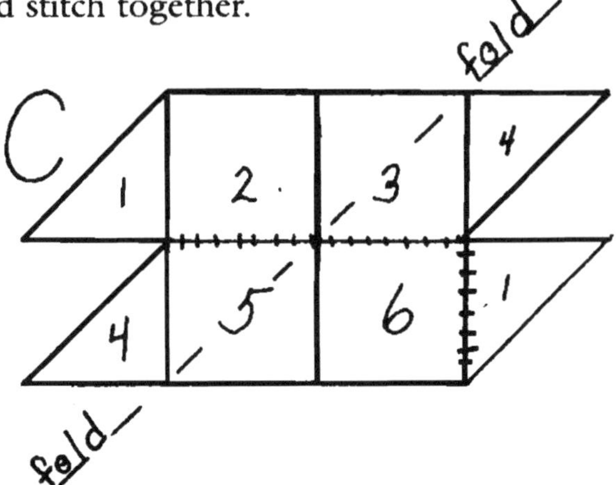

Now fold through #3 and #5, parallel with the diagonally cut ends. To fold through #2 and #6 won't work so remember all these diagonals are going the same way.

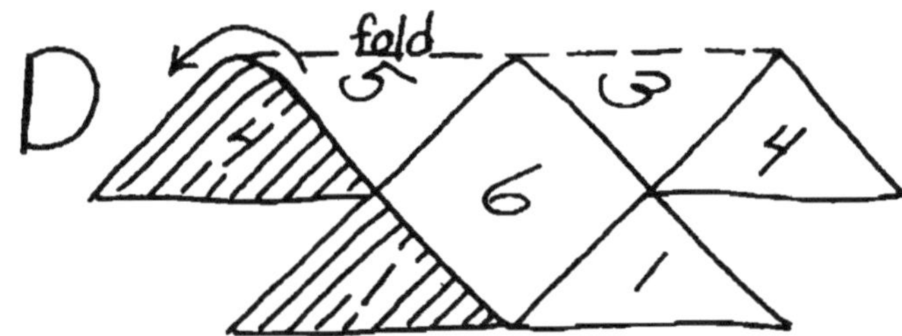

Fold the front #1 around to the back, the back #1 around to the front. The diagonal edges of #1 touch the edges of #6 and #2. Fold the lower edges of the #4 triangles so they touch #3 on the right, #5 on the left. Fold the little tips of #4 again so they touch themselves. You have a top with sleeves tapered at the wrist. Try this yourself to see how beautifully it works.

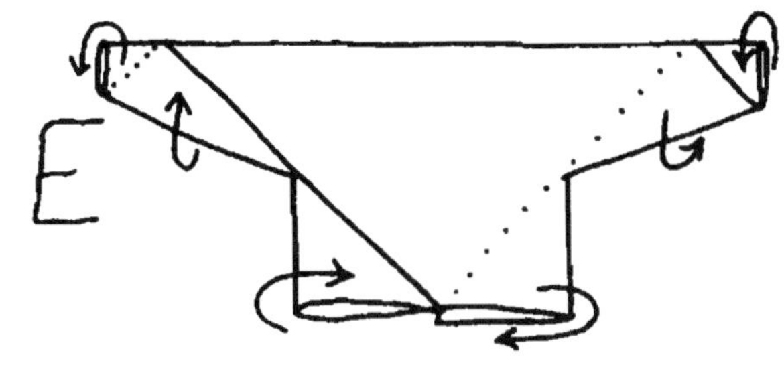

The only thing this lacks is a neckline and that would be done in step **C** before folding begins or after **E**, which ever you chose. Also after **E** the touching edges are stitched together to become a garment. As you might imagine, the easiest time for a neckline is right after attaching the two rows together, in diagram **C**.

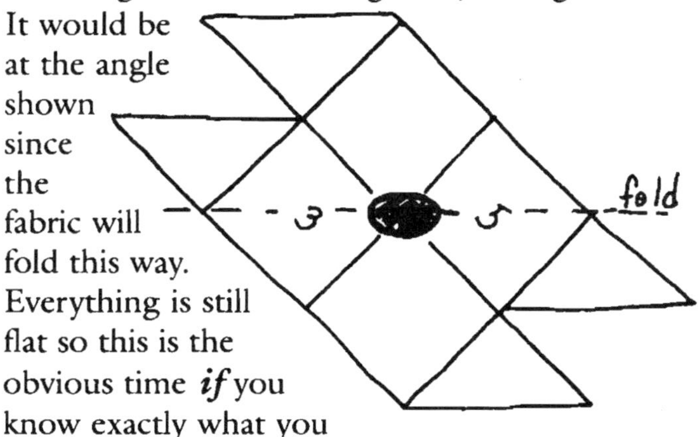

It would be at the angle shown since the fabric will fold this way. Everything is still flat so this is the obvious time *if* you know exactly what you want to do. I was still trying to figure out what this "simple" garment was all about, so held off until later. Obviously it will be less convenient to cut and finish the neckline when the garment is sewn together and is in the round.

Use the chart at the end of this chapter to determine the size of your 6 squares. Notice that in step **D** the diagonal of a square from point to point is how wide the finished garment will be. This is the front of the garment, therefore one-half its size. Twice that width will be the whole garment. Notice that it will be as long as it is wide. In other words, the body of this top is a square with sleeves projecting from it – a **T** shaped top.

Figure the circumference needed in bust or if long enough in hips also. If this will be too short or too long, add a band or fold up a hem. Put this together with edges only touching and zigzagged together before covering with ribbon, braid, strips of some sort. If actual seams are preferred the squares have to be a little larger to allow for this.

This long strip of fabric is probably going to begin as one piece but it doesn't have to. You can start with six separate squares and put them together as one. In the example I showed on television, I had only enough for five squares in length so I added a sixth square of another fabric. I chose to make that square #1 and in a darker fabric. It appears at the waistline sides. I used inexpensive fabric for a test pattern which is good idea before cutting into precious fabrics.

To detail all the variations and complete instructions chronologically is an impossibility rather like determining whether the chicken or the egg came first. You in general know what this project is all about and the best I can now do is categorize different areas of decision making. They are all interdependent on one another so you'll have to jump back and forth as your personal needs demand.

Fabrics to Use

Because this will all be on the bias, soft fabrics work well and drape nicely. Knits and wovens both are a consideration, handwovens being especially nice. If these wovens have prominent warp yarns producing a striped effect it will emphasize the whole bias idea. Thin, airy mesh fabrics work well, maybe incorporate a ravelled-out fringe. Border prints might be a good idea but first work out in miniature paper form to realize that some of the border will be upside down. If this matters, rethink your idea.

Expensive fabrics can be nicely used here as such a small amount is needed. Narrow fabrics can be utilized for this project since the narrow widths will be spiral-stitched into a larger garment than one would suspect. Supplemental strips can be added to increase size.

What fabrics would be senseless for this? Firmly woven solid fabrics are better used on the straight. Suedes, leathers, dense fabrics wouldn't work advantageously. This styling really is best in soft, loose, drapey fabrics which beg to be cut on the bias and softly envelop the body.

Cutting and Seaming

There are three seams in this. The initial one when you sew the two rows together in **figure C**. The little #1 triangle stitched in figure B could have been by-passed – I'll tell you how later. Seams #2 and #3 are illustrated in figure E when everything folds around and comes together.

Your first cutting and seaming decision will be where you are going to sew seams together with seam allowances? These will have to be added to the original measurements. The other alternative is to just butt edges together, zigzag to join, then cover up the joining with strips such as ribbons, bias tapes, braids, suede or leather strips. Whatever covers and reinforces the joining in an attractive way will be just fine.

To line up this joining in figure **C**, the placement is obvious. One row simply goes below the other row, matching up the squares.

Back up to figure **B**, however. There are many instances where I don't want that **#1** triangle stitched onto the end of **#6** in an obvious joining. Eliminate this if you want. Why not put the top of **#1** on **#6** *before* cutting out. Instead of a row of six squares, turn it into a parallelogram at the outset. This doesn't waste any fabric as you can still get bias strips on each end for binding the neckline, etc.

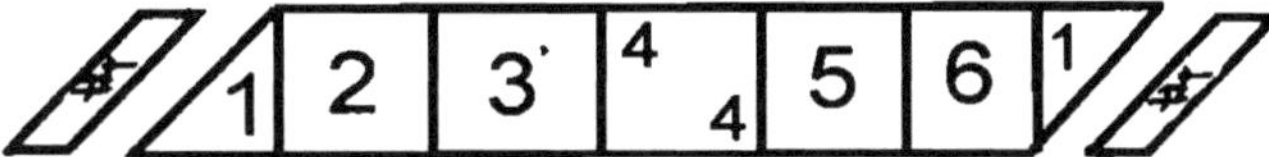

In some fabrics you would be better off with seam allowances rather than zigzagging. This must be planned in advance as the seam allowances will need a little more fabric. To make it easy let's use $\frac{1}{2}$" seam allowances. This illustration shows with the dark lines where they'll be added

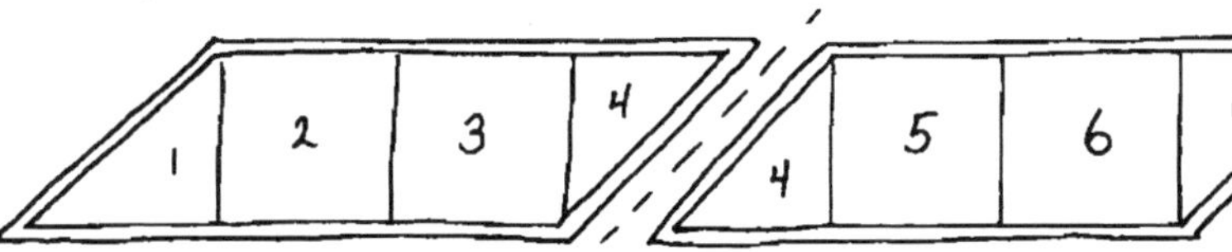

– or depending on when you add **#1** triangle.

When the two rows are stitched together, stitch only the actual squares leaving the $\frac{1}{2}$" seam allowance at ends unstitched.

When the remaining two major stitching lines are connected in diagram **E**, begin at the waistline, the big open area. Then pin and stitch your way around the spiral to the sleeve, the

small area. This is do-able. The reverse is not. Notice the diagonal edges of **#4** will be stitched to the straight stable of **#3** and **#5** squares, nicely holding it all in shape. The diagonal edges of **#1** will be the lower edge so stability is not an issue.

When instead of seam allowances you are zigzagging edges together in those three major joinings, serge any raw edges first to secure edges keeping them more sturdy and safe from raveling. Set your zigzag stitch at its widest to grasp each edge as securely as possible. An easy way to pin these edges together first so they all match up properly is to use the curved quilters' safety pins. Form the bodice spiral around a rotary cutting mat so you can easily pin edges without connecting the front and back. Remove the pins as you machine stitch up to them.

Neckline Ideas

As mentioned, the best time to do the neckline is probably in figure **C** as soon as the two rows are stitched together. The placement of its template would be as the center **X** with its square numbers indicates. The equivalent of shoulder seams would be on the fold line **S**. Cut out this template oval, then finish the neckline as you like. Refer to the oval/template at the top of the next page.

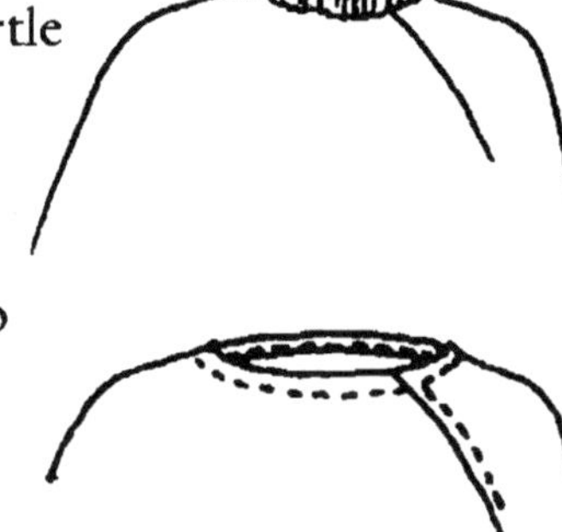

Maybe a narrow bias binding would be suitable. This would need a further opening to slip your head through. A logical place for this would be in the seam that slants down to the left, perhaps with button loops to button together.

If a knit, cut the neckline a little larger and stitch a ribbing for a mock turtle or crew neck.

Cut it wider still for a boat neckline and your head will slip through without an additional opening.

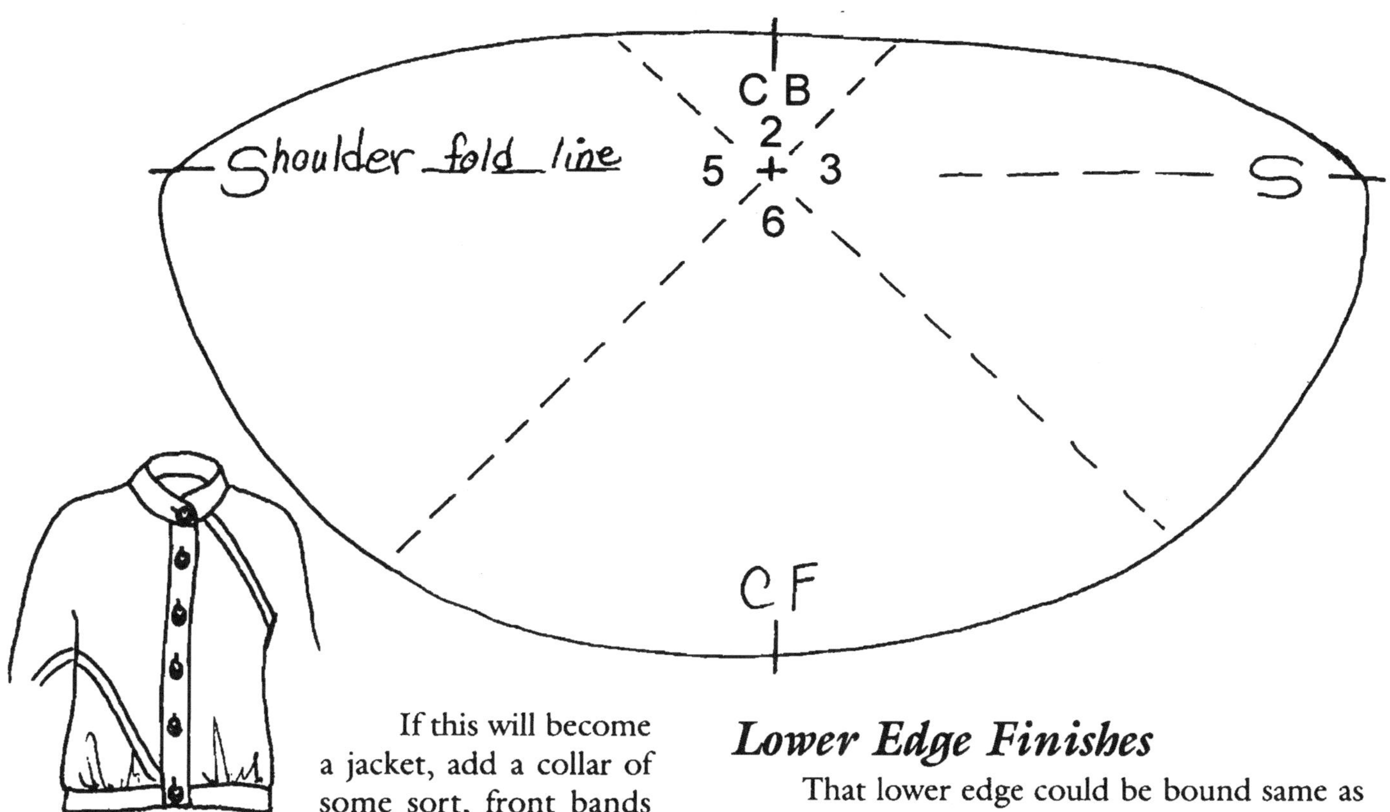

If this will become a jacket, add a collar of some sort, front bands for buttons and button-holes, and a lower band.

Lengthening The Bodice

If the jacket just mentioned or if some sort of a belted top is your preference, a longer hemline is needed. As is, the bodice part turns out a square. Accommodate this while cutting out by lengthening square #1 on each end. As the two rows are stitched together, notice how the #1 triangles extend beyond #4. When finished those bias cut ends hang down longer.

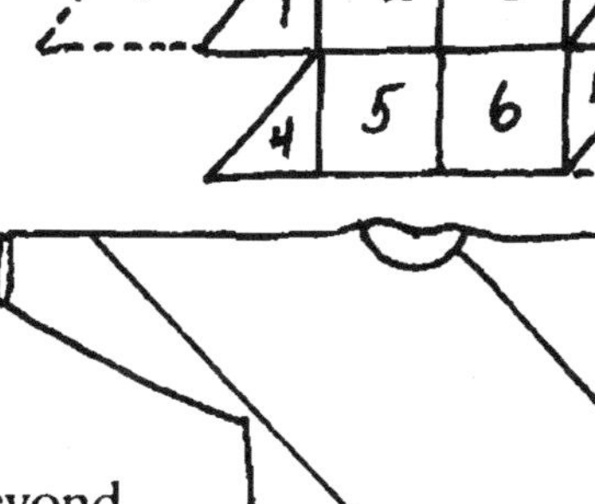

Lower Edge Finishes

That lower edge could be bound same as the neckline. Another alternative would be to hem it up in shallow machine top stitching after first serging the raw bias edge. A separate facing might be still another choice. Any of these might encase elastic or a drawstring.

Expanding Narrow Fabric

Some fabrics (hand woven or Japanese imports) are woven in quite narrow widths and may be too narrow to produce the size squares you need. Find a harmonizing fabric and sew straight strips on the top and bottom at the outset to widen as necessary. Remember if you widen you'll also lengthen to keep these squares.

There are endless twists and turns, many variations in this origami top that we could expand on forever. By now you have a grasp of the situation and can imagine a wealth of other possibilities. Enjoy your personal creations!

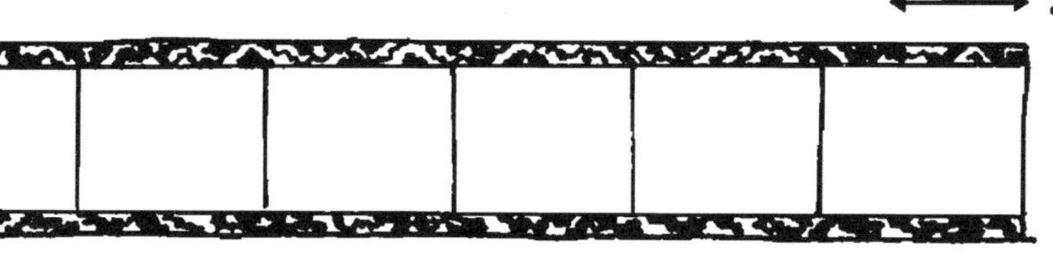

Origami Top Fabric Chart

if square is	garment circumference	garment length	45" or 60" yardage needed	narrow fabric needed
10"	28$\frac{1}{2}$"	14$\frac{1}{4}$"	5/8 yd	60"
11"	31$\frac{1}{4}$"	15$\frac{5}{8}$"	5/8	66"
12"	34"	17"	2/3	72"
13"	37"	18$\frac{1}{2}$"	3/4	78"
14"	39$\frac{3}{4}$"	19$\frac{7}{8}$"	7/8	84"
15"	42$\frac{1}{2}$"	21$\frac{1}{4}$"	7/8	90"
16"	45$\frac{1}{4}$"	22$\frac{5}{8}$"	1	96"
17"	48"	24"	1	102"
18"	51"	25$\frac{1}{2}$"	1	108"
19"	54"	27"	1 1/8	114"
20"	56$\frac{1}{2}$"	28$\frac{1}{4}$"	1 1/8	120"
21"	59$\frac{1}{2}$"	29$\frac{3}{4}$"	1 1/4	126"
22"	62$\frac{1}{2}$"	31$\frac{1}{4}$"	1 1/4	132"

Gray Skies

You keep asking me where does my inspiration come from? Where do I get my ideas? The answer is everywhere. One thought drifts into another reminding me of something in my collection. As I look through fabrics and trims things begin to gel into a solid whole.

For example, one night Madam Butterfly was showing on television and I became interested in her costume changes. All kimonos, but the styling was different in each. I decided to translate one of them into a vest, and this became ***Element #1 Kimono Styled Vest.***

That reminded me that I had purchased many small pieces of kimono silk. These garments had been worn many times. Some entrepreneur gathered them together, ripped out the seams, cut them into smaller pieces and sold them. I found them in a big bin in a booth at a consumer sewing show. Each were neatly folded in zip lock bags. The largest of these was about 16" square, but many were smaller. As I sorted through the collection I chose pieces with some red in the print. The prints were all different but the red was the common link to tie them together in some way, perhaps a solid fabric of rocky road type piecing. That was my thinking at the time of purchase ... which usually changes before actually making the fabric into some garment. This became ***Element #2 Little Silk Print Pieces.***

As I removed them each from their bags to sort out and inspect, many alternatives came to me other than the piecing. Most had floral prints, some intermingled with geometric or curvy lines. I began to see them as appliqué rather than as a pieced fabric, perhaps cutting them into butterflies dancing through space. Another had a tassel print and I thought of appliquéed fans connected by silk cords and real tassels. On one I discovered a truly unique print: a tiny Japanese lady surrounded by tiny umbrellas.

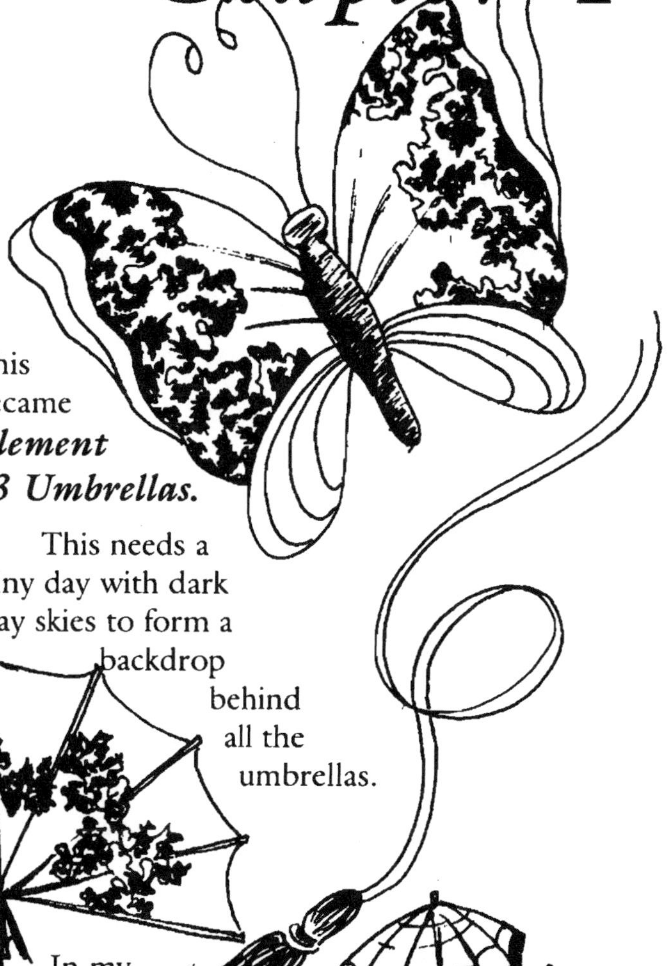

This became ***Element #3 Umbrellas.***

This needs a rainy day with dark gray skies to form a backdrop behind all the umbrellas.

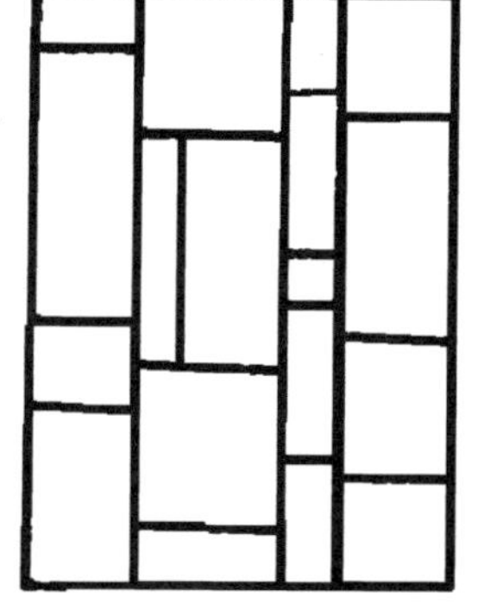

In my "resource center" there is an entire gray shelf in lighter or darker tints and shades. One of these was a soft crepe, perfect for a long-sleeved blouse and pants plus the vest since there was a sufficient supply of it. This became ***Element #4 Gray Skies***

All this needed an excuse for being. What's a rainy day unless you have something that resembles rain? Perhaps my drawers of yarn and novelty threads would have something useful, and there it was! A novelty thin cord had a big chenille dot about every inch in variegated bright colors. Applied in streaks at an angle is ***Element #5 Rain.***

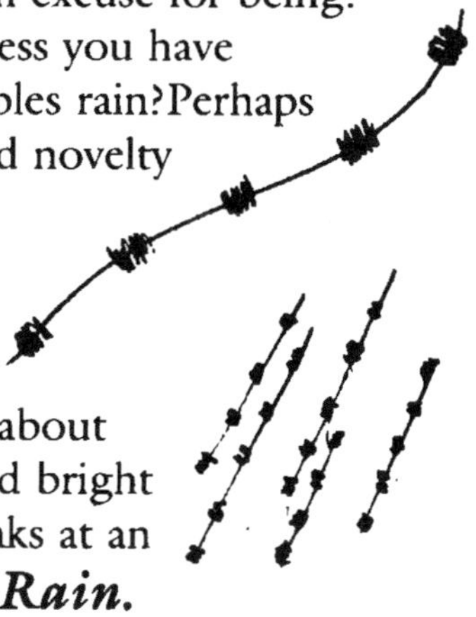

Approached in this way, every garment I make almost designs itself. Everything relates to something else – I just can't wait to get started. Sewing is so rewarding, I could spend forever in my sewing room and never run out of entertainment.

I still needed a way to put it all together. With dozens of umbrellas to appliqué I didn't want to turn under all those little curved edges. Stitching it to a backing fabric, clipping every edge frequently, turning right side out, pressing would be another alternatve – also rejected. A third idea: simply cut out the shapes and fuse them to the backing fabric. The raw edges need some treatment however, and satin stitching each outline sounds like a two-day job. Then my old friend, black illusion – the very thin netting – popped into my mind. Cover the whole project with a layer of it over the umbrellas to protect all the raw edges from wear. Stitch all the "rain" over that to quilt layers together and the whole mixture of ideas has jelled.

The thought of gray skies may not sound cheerful to everyone unless you haven't had rain and need it badly. By now I was elated and only saw the bright side, the silver lining. Let's celebrate with a whole parade of these colorful umbrellas. If you can't draw people it really doesn't matter. As you look out in a crowded area on a rainy day, the people are hidden under the umbrellas. All that would show are the rounded umbrella shapes – easy enough for everyone.

For the garment shape, find a drop-shouldered tee shirt pattern you undoubtedly have. Leave the sleeves off, just using the front and back bodice pieces. I shaped in the waistline slightly to eliminate some bulk since it would be belted. This will be a wrap front so the center front edge will be brought down to a V and extended to

overlap a few inches. Mme. Butterfly had a collar on hers as pictured. For this cut a rectangle 8" x 18" on the bias (to fold over more softly). Fold this in half lengthwise, stitch the ends, turn right side out and press. Raw edges of the collar are enclosed between the vest outside and lining layers as they are stitched together. This I did on trial fabric to be sure it gave the desired effect before cutting on expensive fabric. The trial vest is wearable and goes nicely over the gray pant outfit, so no effort was wasted. I decided against the collar. On my final project with umbrellas, there is a band going all around the front and neck edge. This is a straight cut strip $3\frac{1}{2}$" wide and as long as the garment edge. Another strip the same width forms the belt, long enough to tie in a front bow.

The simple umbrella pattern on the previous page (and last page of this chapter) doesn't use a handle. I only drew this once, in a small size. I wanted four sizes. The others are identical, each traced $\frac{1}{4}$" or so larger each time.

Since these would be fused, then stitched over, be sure to use a light weight fusible rather than a heavy duty one that can't be stitched through. These paper backed fusibles are thin enough to cut several layers at once to save time. All these cut-outs are then ready to fuse to the back sides of the appliqué fabrics.

A great surface for doing this job is the large size Space Board from HTC. This is a padded board 51" x 33" that covers most of my cutting table when in use. It folds in half, handles on each side for out of the way storage. On this I put all the little fabric pieces, wrong side up. The print design shows through the fabric so I could see where I was placing each umbrella before fusing it down. The designs seemed to invite placement. Balls like this perfectly accommodate the umbrella shapes. On others, flowers seemed to be made to border the scalloped umbrella edge. This was most enjoyable finding just the right placement.

As you know, I do my own work rather than hiring a sewing room staff. The exception is when it comes to tasks that are repetitious, boring, and takes no expertise to do. For this I await my opportunity. When John (hubby) sits down to watch a ball game on TV I can always talk him into cutting out whatever is needed. I was most grateful for the 50 umbrellas from his scissors! What a gem!

I arranged the umbrellas on the vest pieces, again using the padded Space Board. The larger umbrellas on the bottom, smaller ones on top to look like a farther distance. They curve back and forth to look like a parade going up a curvy path on a hill. Begin at the top and progress to the bottom overlapping each slightly, tilting them back and forth, perpendicular to the path. Peel off the paper backings before placing so when you like the placement, you can fuse with your steam iron.

I decided to put a layer of cotton flannel (**preshrink before cutting out**) under my gray crepe. On top of the umbrella appliqués went the layer of black illusion. It covers everything without obscurring the design, only slightly toning down the bright colors.

With a yardstick and powdered chalk wheel, draw a few parallel lines at a slant similar to the slant of wind-driven rain. I made some of these shorter, some longer, with variable spacing between. It becomes more interesting than having everything at regular intervals. Using monofilament thread that is invisible, the "rain" is then zigzagged in place over the chalk lines, maybe adding a few extra streaks here and there. Which foot used for this depends on your equipment and the yarn or cords being couched in place. I found a clear plastic foot easiest to see exactly what was happening. It also had a flat cutout channel under the foot which perfectly accommodated the chenille slubs.

That pretty silk scrap with the umbrella lady that inspired this garment is satin stitched to the lining inside the back neck. She doesn't even show when the vest is worn, but to have some special touch inside a garment just adds to the feeling of satisfaction in your completed project.

Any little scraps of that print silk? Use them for something fun like little Japanese kimonos filled with a combination of fiberfill and sachet. They're marvelous little treasures to have in your drawers, closets or make delightful hostess gifts. Use atop a gift box instead of a bow.

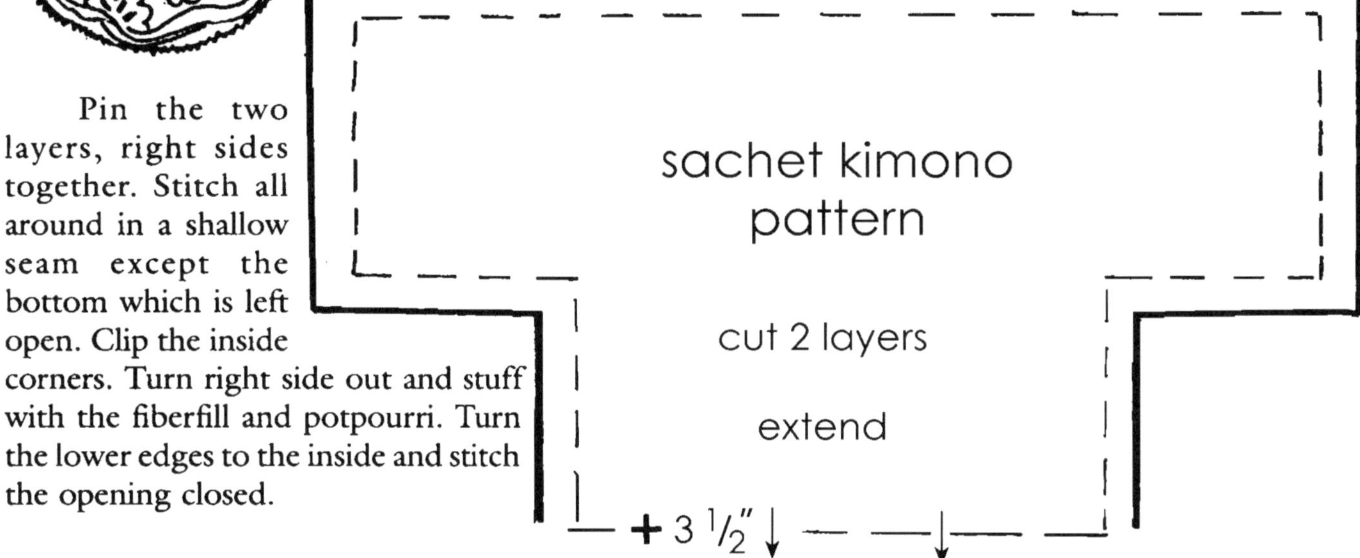

Pin the two layers, right sides together. Stitch all around in a shallow seam except the bottom which is left open. Clip the inside corners. Turn right side out and stuff with the fiberfill and potpourri. Turn the lower edges to the inside and stitch the opening closed.

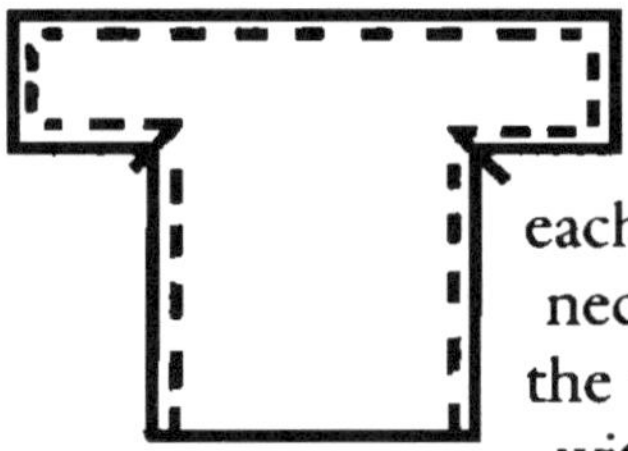

Tie a ribbon in a bow around it under the arms and it makes a charming little pretty. Next time you'll be with a little group of friends, make one to give to each. They're fun and any kind of print fabric will do – silk isn't necessary. Next Christmas consider making several to hang on the tree, pine sachet used as stuffing. Hang a few in the kitchen with herbs or spices as stuffing. Just make something pretty to turn your gray skies sunny.

Water Colors   Chapter 5

We're dealing with sheer fabrics, but those on this program happened to be in the blues and greens of water colors. Think of that watery quality – transparent – and that quality presents some alternative techniques where choices must be made.

For starters, these fabrics whether silk or polyester are usually quite slippery and it's a very rare shop that cuts them straight. I always buy a little more than I need to allow for straightening. Typically the cut edge looks something like this, wavering higher or lower in spots.

You should be able to ravel one yarn of the fabric all the way across. This is known as being thread perfect. Find the lowest spot, pull up the yarn (thread) that edges it and pull it out to the selvage on each side. It will leave a bare path on which you can cut

a straight line. If the yarns are weak and break, they still produce a series of wrinkles all the way along. Cut as far as you can on the wrinkle marks, then pick up a new thread and pull it repeating the process until you have cut a thread perfect edge all across.

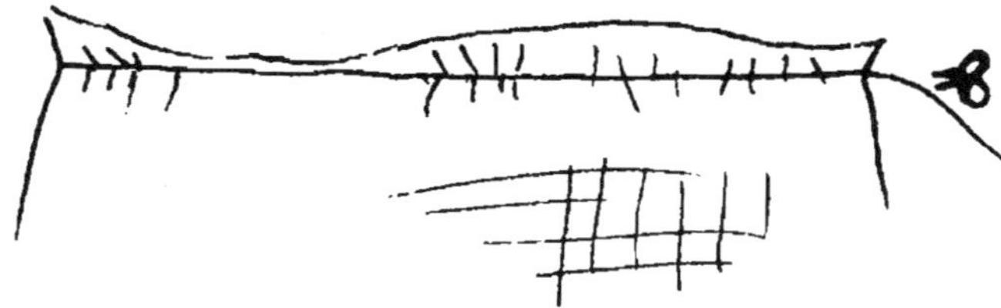

Before cutting out the garment decisions must be made. In a fashion magazine you'll see the one transparent layer in a blouse with nothing worn under it. On real women we consider another layer to make it opaque. That extra layer could be a lining attached to the blouse bodice of an equally thin fabric. Another choice is to wear the one-layer blouse over a camisole or a sleeveless shell. If the garment is a sleeveless shell of sheer fabric, consider making it two layers of sheer, two colors or a print and a solid. Attached at all edges or the lower edges hemmed separately, it can expand your wardrobe as a reversible – two garments in one.

Sleeves on sheer blouses are usually left as one layer. Here the transparency doesn't matter. If there are collars and cuffs, buttonhole and button areas, these often have three layers of the sheer fabric rather than a core layer of interfacing.

If a sheer blouse has a shoulder yoke, treat it this way to machine stitch it all, no later hand stitching or machine topstitching needed. Cut two layers of the yoke. Right sides facing each other, line up the yoke edges sandwiching the blouse back upper edge in between. Stitch a $5/8$" seam. Trim the seam allowances to $1/4$", and press the yoke pieces up. Now drop the yoke

lining layer back down, so that all you see on your table is the *right* side of the blouse back and one yoke layer, raw seam edges underneath.

Position on top of this the two blouse fronts, right sides *down*. Temporarily pin shoulders of the fronts to the yoke edges. I like to do this on my Space Board so I have a big padded surface to stick these pins into, holding everything down securely.

Roll up the blouse fronts and back so they're on the yoke section. Fold up that lower yoke lining piece to cover. Pin the shoulders of the yokes and blouse fronts together. At the machine, stitch shoulder seams and trim to $1/4$".

Turn right side out through the open ends. Press. Proceed with the rest of the construction.

Seams are the next consideration. The easiest seam is on your serger. The 4-thread stitches a secure seam while enclosing the two raw edges. An alternative is a 3-thread rolled seam. This is the same as a rolled hem using the proper adjustment or attachment your serger needs. It gives a narrow seam, but it is strong since the fabric rolls around the stitch finger and encloses the raw edges within the roll. These are especially useful if the seam is quite shaped or curved as opposed to being straight.

French seams are always good on sheers, often seen on expensive ready-to-wear unless it's a very curvy stitching line. Here it couldn't be done as it must turn inside out, perhaps presenting a problem. Stitch first a $3/_8$"seam with the *wrong* fabric sides together. Trim this off short. Press the seam allowances to one side, then turn wrong side out. Press flat and stitch a $1/_4$" seam. The raw edges will be enclosed and this looks the most expensive if the fabric is quite transparent. If just a slight curve, as would be in the sleeve cap of a drop shouldered garment, this should work out. If the sleeve is a high, standard cap, maybe not. Use another alternative.

Still another choice is to stitch a seam, trim it off short. Bind it with a roll of narrow sheer tricot tape. Usually about $1/_2$" wide it is sold in packages and called Seams Great or Seam Saver. This was used more extensively before sergers, but is still a possibility. A slight zigzag stitch in attaching it will insure that the upper and lower edges are both securely caught.

For hems there is again a serger rolled hem, especially good for a big flared skirt. On your sewing machine a rolled hem requires a rolled hem foot. Whatever your brand, it will be available at your dealer. It rolls the fabric over twice before stitching a little $1/_8$" edge. Be sure to do this with the right side down as opposed to a serger where the right side would be up since the stitch finger makes the fabric edge roll under.

Expensive blouses are usually hemmed with a slightly wider hem – about $3/_8$". To get this perfect, run a $5/_8$" from the edge stitching line. At the ironing board press on this line to the underside. Half of that width press under again and machine stitch at the fold edge.

Any of these could be used if making sheer scarves. Notice, though, on the more expensive ones that they always have a hand rolled hem stitched with a finer thread.

To bind the neckline of a scoop-necked shell or a jewel-necked blouse, cut a long bias strip. Depending on the fabric weight this can either be like bias tape, each edge folded in or it could be cut wider and doubled. Either way, the raw edges of it and the neckline will be stitched together in a shallow seam, right sides together. The fold then wraps around to the backside. When you stitch it down in the seam well (the ditch), the stitching line is quite invisible. On the backside the stitches show close to the folded edge of the binding. Either of these can also fold completely to the backside and be

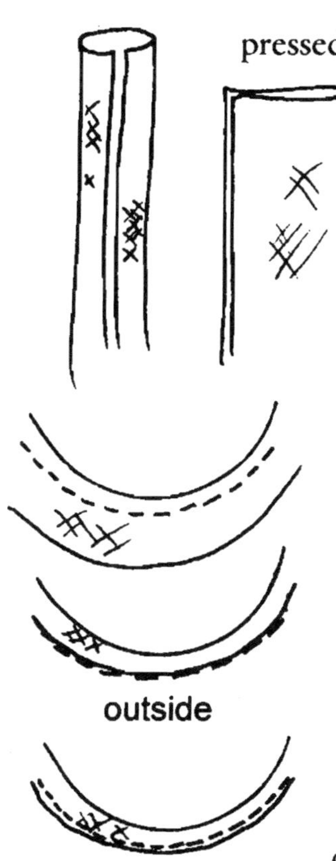

outside

inside

pressed flat after stitching near the bias edge.

Layering these sheer fabrics and quilting them can be quite lovely for vests or jackets. Simply back them with fleece, flannel, or something with a little loft. Most of these backings would be white and try the sheer fabric over it first to see the effect. It will be considerably lighter in color. If you want it to retain its original color, choose a backing of the same color. This eliminates a fleece unless it would be a thin polar fleece – a polyester which comes in a large color assortment. This might make a warmer garment than you might have planned, but it wouldn't be too unlike the fleece purchased in the interfacing department. For a lighter weight, a cotton flannel of the right color might work better. Preshrink that in a hot washer and dryer before cutting out.

In my vest I used something perhaps unorthodox, but it gave the effect I wanted. It was a cotton interlock in a medium weight (tee shirt knit fabric) and the blue-green color of the sheer. Mixing layers of knit and woven? Why not, since they will be quilted together eliminating the stretch anyway. It gives the right color, the right loft, the right effect.

To quilt this I put the two layers in a hoop centering the very slight design of the sheer fabric print. That design looks almost like ripples in water and it seemed logical to just repeat the idea in stitches. Metallic thread would give some sparkle, like water, but I was going to put some etched beads on it and glitzy thread wouldn't be compatible. Rayon thread in blue-green was

therefore used on top, any color can be used in the bobbin since lining would cover it. It will need an embroidery foot and a lowered feed dog since this is free-motion stitching.

Time-consuming but extremely easy to get a pretty effect. Lower the presser foot and stitch a few stitches in a circle just to connect, then stop and cut off the thread end. Go ahead and quilt the whole hoop full. I found it easy to hold only the little hoop handle in one hand to move it from side to side, occasionally making small circles here and there for a little interesting emphasis. Move the hoop to another area and repeat until the fabric is all quilted.

I stitched the shoulder and side seams and tried on the vest. Much to my dismay it didn't even meet in the center, let alone overlap! Not the faintest clue as to how I miss-cut, it happens – move on. Consider the options on how you can turn a time-consuming disaster into something not only wearable, but actually something you like a lot. Remember, when you sew you never truly make a mistake – only provide yourself with a creative opportunity. What to create? A little quilted piece for the right side only that would bridge the gap and fasten to the left side.

That piece was cut with an irregular edge somewhat like the quilting stitch lines. It is attached to the right vest front with a little piping to separate, since there wasn't a fabric scrap left whose printed design would precisely match up. When you can't camouflage it, flaunt it! Then the piping stood out too much, so I decided the answer would be repetition – more vertical lines. These are in the form of bias cut 23 fabric tubes stitched and turned right side out over a Fasturn. These are all stitched in the upper edge seam and freely swing with movement, lower ends weighted by large sea-glass beads. These big beads had a large enough hole in the center to pull the tube through, using needle and strong thread knotted to the tube end. Tie a knot at the end of the fabric tube to hold the big bead in place. A crushed self-fabric waist and tied in the center completes the look. I just love the challenge of turning an ugly toad into a handsome prince!

Tiny beads, seed or bugle beads are sometimes used very effectively on a sheer fabric. I just saw a beautiful strapless formal that had many rows of bugle beads in horizontal rows across the bodice. I have no use for such a gown in my lifestyle, but the *idea* can be transferred to something I can use. For example, a two-piece deep purple suede rayon dress is meant for daytime wear. For that once-in-a-blue-moon dressy occasion I might make a vest of sheer purple chiffon in a flared version, rows and rows of these beads (can be purchased by the yard) zigzagged on with monofilament thread.

A gray crepe pant outfit would turn very dressy with a sheer longer vest, same bead treatment for a shimmery evening look. Small accessory, major effect. Explore your closet to find something old to update with a new piece.

These sheers are so elegant layered, experiment to see what else can be done. A few shapes randomly cut in various colors could be laid on the base fabric. Cover it over with your sheer top layer and hold in place with pins. Quilt over the top of this for lovely results.

Think about doing this for other reasons. Perhaps you have a fabric in a bold print whose impact you would like to soften. To cover it with a cheer fabric, then quilt can tone it down to something more appealing with a richer depth.

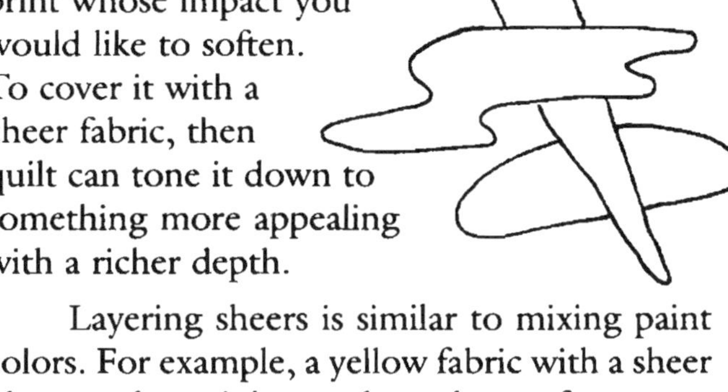

Layering sheers is similar to mixing paint colors. For example, a yellow fabric with a sheer blue overlay might produce the perfect green to go with another garment. That same blue over red would become purple, etc. Experiment for some lovely surprises.

Antique fabrics can benefit by this overlay idea. If they are weakened and might disintegrate if used alone, mount them on a thin, sturdy backing to begin the process. Putting a sheer overlay on top safely sandwiches them between so the design, piecing, whatever will show through but be protected.

Working with these sheers can be a sheer delight and an experience you ought to try.

Handler Textile Corporation

Deep Purple Chapter 6

"When I'm an old woman I shall wear purple" – so the poem goes. Purple is one of my favorite colors. I started wearing it when I was very young so won't ever have to admit to growing old. Plan ahead!

Sewing requires planning to make everything turn out just right. Sometimes you anticipate what problems you'll encounter and weigh the alternatives, selecting the best solution. Other times you don't know there is a problem until you're in the midst of it. But the beauty of sewing is that there are always many solutions, many ways to do any given technique.

The purple faux leather jacket being worked on during this program is an exact copy of a magazine photo. When you sew you can have anything you want. By making slight changes in a basic pattern, anything you see or imagine can easily be done. The difference between sewing it yourself and buying it is that you don't have the limited choices offered on ready-to-wear racks. You choose the style, the fabric, the fit and every other minute detail you prefer to produce exactly what you want. I can't imagine accepting anything less.

Even though this is a manmade leather, the same challenges would occur in synthetic suede as well as in closely woven fabrics. The fabric is so dense that you can only ease in a very limited amount without having any puckers show. The place this most commonly presents a problem is in the sleeve cap. A scant 1" of excess might be eased into a 10" area. This is about the distance from the front notch to the back notches in a standard set-in sleeve. The problem is that the sleeve cap at the stitching line is $1\frac{1}{2}$" up to 2" larger than the armscye into which you will set that sleeve. To ease in the whole amount with its resultant puckers looks unbearably homemade and that look can't be tolerated. Here are some alternatives.

Years ago it was common on these fabrics to just trim off some of the sleeve cap at the top. True, it would then measure less and also true, it would ease in smoothly. The only trouble

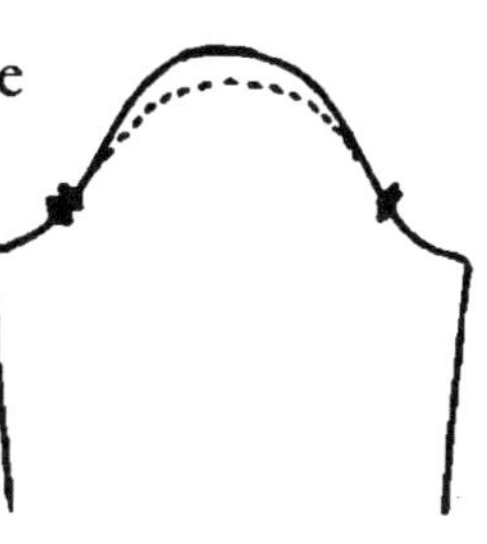

is that a well fitting sleeve should hang smoothly with your arm down at your side. That excess fabric at the cap allows it to round out nicely and provide the proper cap length. Obviously, to trim some length will alter the picture. With your arm hanging normally you would see diagonal wrinkles form back and front, pointing up to the problem: a too-short sleeve cap. To make those wrinkles disappear hold out your arm and the sleeve is again smooth. But you can hardly walk around with extended arms so this is not a good solution.

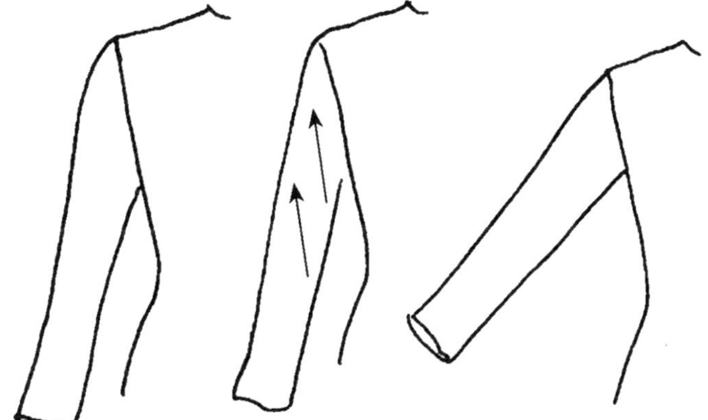

Another alternative some have suggested is to cut the bodice armscye down lower under the arm and the sleeve will then fit this enlarged armscye. Check out the wisdom of this right now: Reach over to the under sleeve area of what you are wearing. Grasp the undersleeve down a way from the underarm seam and hold the sleeve against your body. Try to move that arm and you will experience a definite restriction in freedom of movement. It's a little like being bound into a straight jacket, so we can also eliminate this idea. Sewing is mostly common sense and to think your way through alternatives leads you to feasible solutions. Let's find a few ways that actually work.

To insert the sleeve in the armscye begin at the underarm point. This will be either a seam or, if a side panel, a dot on the pattern will indicate the location. There is really no easing in under the arm so merely pin the sleeve (right side out) to the jacket (wrong side out), pins on the sleeve side. I use .5mm pins because when they're this fine they don't leave marks in the fabric as larger ones would. Pin parallel to the fabric edge so when all pinned, the garment can be tried on to make sure the placement is just right before stitching. Next pin at the shoulder point. All the easing takes place where the curved arrows are located. On a woven fabric this would be bias, and works in more easily than straight grain. On the suedes and leather this doesn't apply, but still this is the position of easing. As you pin from the notches up toward the top, any sleeve fabric in excess can just be folded over as shown. This produces a little tuck in front of and behind the shoulder seam, and provides an attractive design feature.

Another way to eliminate some cap excess is to make a series of twin-needle pintucks. About $1\frac{1}{2}$" inches long, they provide needed roundness at the cap as well as being quite interesting. At the lower end of each stitching line pull the thread ends to the sleeve inside and tie knots. To backstitch it would show and look bad. On the same garment consider making self-fabric covered buttons

with the same tucking technique. Depending on how many tucks you stitch, a lot of excess fabric can be eliminated from the cap.

The method I used on the plum leather sleeve on this program involved making a curved dart right at the shoulder point. With the sleeve folded inside out pin, then stitch the dart perhaps $3\frac{1}{2}$" long. A straight dart won't do as it eliminates the roundness a cap needs. Stitching this curve eliminates as much extra fabric as is needed at the stitching line. It tapers to an elongated, slim point with no bulge at its tip.

Slash open this dart as far as is possible with some little scissors in order to press the seam open. A curved surface is necessary for a good job. A tailor's ham can be purchased inexpensively in a fabric store notions and small equipment department. It usually has one side of cotton drill the other side of a wool flannel. Use the flannel side up. Find a place on it where the dart curves in the same shape. Open the dart, cover it with a press cloth, and steam press on the stitching line. Remove the iron and press cloth. Work it a little flatter still with your fingers while it is still warm and steamy. It flattens beautifully. When set into the armscye the dart looks like a continuation of the bodice shoulder seam and is quite attractive.

There are still other ways to eliminate some excess sleeve cap fabric. Maybe you can invent your own workable alternatives.

Another touchy place for proper pressing is at the point of a collar. As you stitch the corner area, make stitches smaller for greater security and take a diagonal stitch or two right at the corner for better turning.

Press the seam open over a point presser, another indispensable piece of equipment. It's wood and ordinarily attached to a clapper or pounding block. That lower platform is an aid to further flatten a just-pressed edge.

The collar point fits over this enabling you to press open the seam as you fit the fabric point on the wood point. Turn the fabric around so each seam is pressed up to its point. Then you are ready to "grade".

Grading is trimming each seam allowance in an enclosed area (such as a collar, cuff, etc.) a different width so the end result will be professional smoothness rather than a stiff ridge. The seam allowance closer to your body is trimmed shorter, about $1/_8$" or a little more for safety's sake. The outer seam allowance is trimmed slightly longer – about $1/_4$". Cut off the corner as close to the stitching line as is safely possible.

The collar is then turned right side out aided by a point turner to get a crisp point. Then on the ironing board press the edge flat with the wrong side up, just slightly rolling the seam to what will be the underside. Again, a press cloth is necessary if a faux suede or leather.

The process for a rounded collar edge is a little different and we'll continue in chapter 7.

Maybe you noticed on this program there was fusible interfacing in the sleeve cap. I sometimes do this if it seems advantageous to give the fabric extra body in the area. Usually the lower edge is cut with pinking shears so it "feathers" into a more invisible blending. Other interfaced areas in a jacket of this sort are the entire fronts. On the side front it will be in an area under the arm and a patch down lower where the slash pocket will be located. The side back will also need the

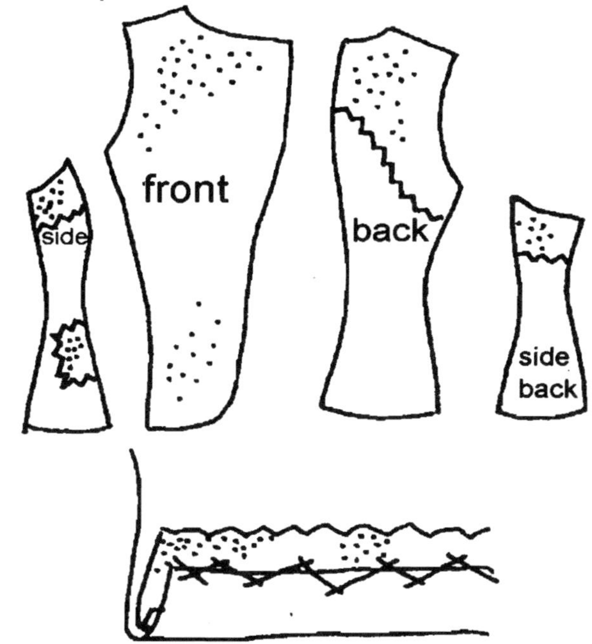

underarm firmness. The center back panel needs the shoulder area interfaced. All hems need a strip which extends above the hem raw edge to cushion so the hem edge can't be seen on the garment outside. It also extends about $1/_2$" at the lower fold into the hem. Catch stitch the hem edge to this interfacing and stitches won't show on the outside. I know it's possible to glue or fuse the hem in place for a quicker job. I always think quality, elegant looks over the long haul. This way it will continue to look marvelous for the life of the garment which will be many years, for these classic garments really don't go out of style. Sometimes the quick methods get to look tacky after a little wear.

Interfacing is not actually pretty, for that is not the intent. It is utilitarian in nature and absolutely makes these garments – a real necessity. My new favorite for this crisply tailored look is Satin Weave by HTC, one of their new couture line. It will all be covered by lining so it will never show when the jacket is finished. Using the fusibles whenever possible (almost all the time) makes the job easier than the sew-ins and takes less expertise to achieve professional looking results. For a more extensive exploration into the interfacing picture, refer to The Sewing Connection, series 16.

Bound buttonholes are perhaps easier to make in leathers and suedes than in any other fabrics. First make the lips not individually, but in long strips. Cut these strips about $3/_4$" to 1" wide and as long as will be needed for the several button holes you will be constructing. Fuse to the backside a strip of lightweight fusible web with the peel-off paper backing.

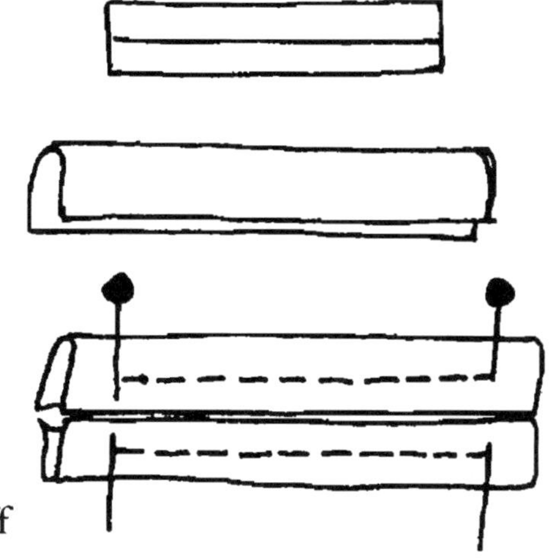

While still warm, peel off the paper, fold the strip in half lengthwise and finger press along its length. It will stick together and stay in this folded position. Cover with a press cloth and press thoroughly with a steam iron. Trim the raw edges off so it is a very uniform $1/4$" in width. This is easier to achieve uniformity than to originally cut it $1/2$" and try to fold such a narrow strip in half. Now cut the strip into pieces, each about 1" longer than the intended buttonhole opening.

Position these so the raw edges touch in the center on the right side of your interfaced garment. Pin on the garment, pins marking the ends of the stitching lines. Stitch exactly down the strip centers, backstitching at each end.

On the jacket wrong side slash through the center between your two stitching lines a *short* distance being careful to cut nothing on the lips sewn on the other side. Slash diagonally out to the end of each stitching line.

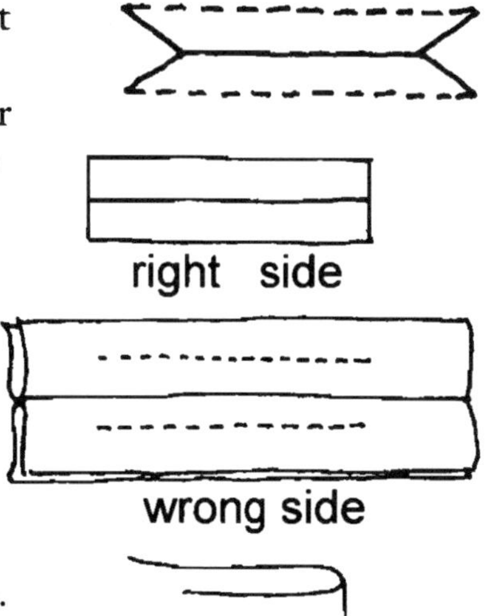

Turn the lips to the backside and finger press in place. The fold edges will now touch in the center, raw edges away from each other.

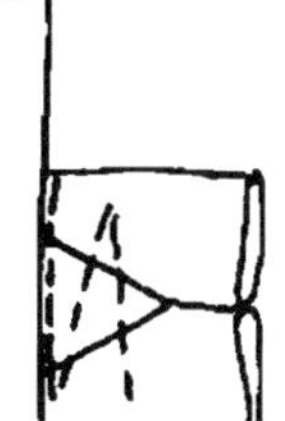

Garment right side up, fold back to the buttonhole end. You will see this under it: the two lip ends covered by the triangle.

Stitch the triangle down to the lip ends. Repeat at the buttonhole other end and you are finished. Lay a strip of brown paper (grocery bag) under each end to prevent impressions showing on the right side. Cover it all with a press cloth and steam press.

Buttonhole will be complete after the facing backs it. Pin layers to hold exactly in place. Stitch in the ditch all around

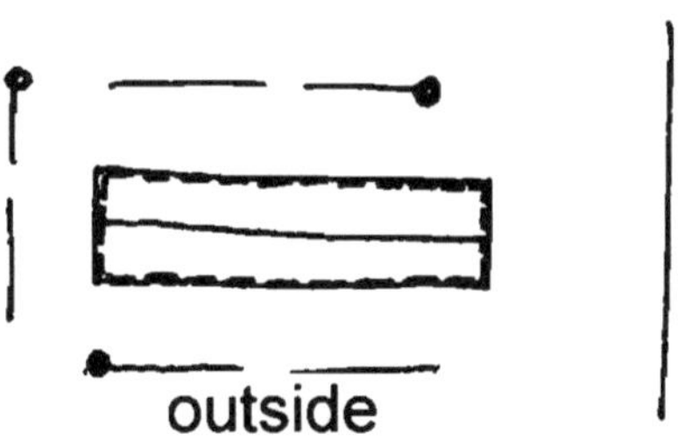

the buttonhole and your stitches won't even show but the facing will be held in place.

On the facing side carefully cut away the facing only, close to the stitching line. This latter process was for suedes and leathers only.

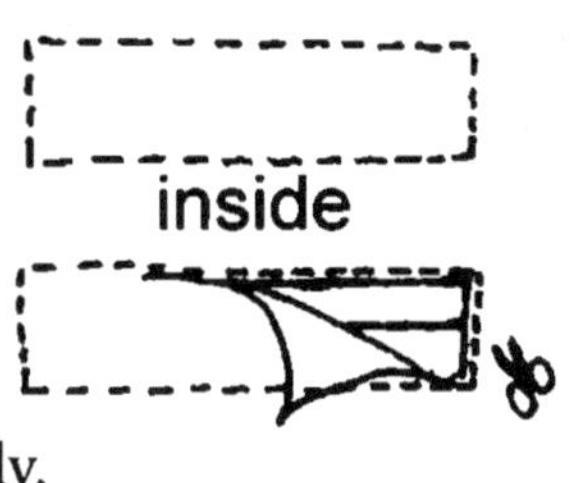

On woven fabrics, again pin all around the buttonhole to hold the facing in place. Stab a pin through each end to mark the place.

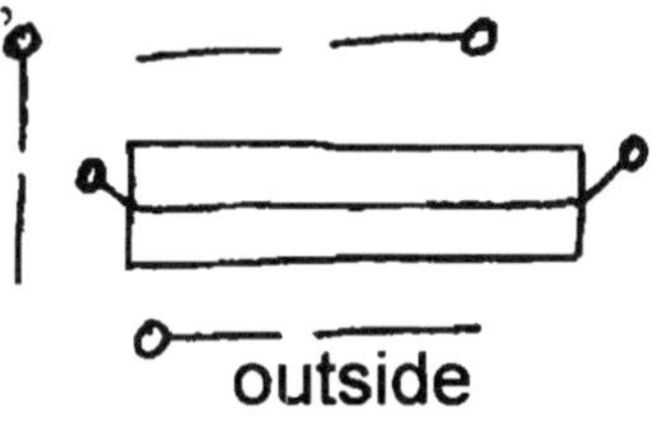

On the facing side carefully cut a slit between the two pins through the facing layer only. Turn under the little facing cut edges and invisibly stitch them down by hand to the buttonhole backside.

Now we've done a little nitty gritty work on these leathers, suedes and tightly woven fabrics. In the next chapter let's move on the fun part – embellishing and finishing touches.

Most of us sew for the fun of it and what I really enjoy is making everything not only as good looking as possible, but also to look distinctive, to have that something extra. These details involve manmade leathers here, but these techniques could just as easily be applied to other fabrics – whatever it is we want to embellish.

Let's pick up from last program where a collar seam and point was pressed open, graded, and pressed closed. Those straight lines are beautifully done with the help of a point presser. The jacket on this program however, a red leather, has a rounded shawl collar. So much for the straight-lined point presser! How can you perfectly finish those enclosed seams that are curvy instead of flat? There are a few ways, but pressing open initially is not the one I would prefer as it can too easily distort the shape.

The first step after stitching the outer seam edge will be grading it. Again, the shorter seam allowance, about $\frac{1}{8}$" will be closer to the body – the undercollar.

The upper collar seam will be slightly longer, a scant $\frac{1}{4}$". As you look at the sketch it would seam like some clipping or notching of that outer curve would be necessary before turning right side out. In reality, they are narrow enough that this is unnecessary and not even a good idea as the hollow places would show in leather. In a ravelly fabric they would be graded a little longer and then might need notching.

Once graded a decision must be made on whether or not to understitch. This is smoothing both seam allowances toward the undercollar and stitching close to the seam. The process insures that the seam is perfectly flat and will nicely

roll to the underside. After this understitching it is easy to place the collar on the ironing board, undercollar side up and press. This is the best way if no topstitching will be done on the right side.

If there will be topstitching I'd prefer to bypass the understitch. Instead, if this is a woven or knit fabric I might even baste this in place (with a fine silk thread so no pressing impressions remain) then press. After pressing do your topstitching, one or two rows, and pull out the basting line before pressing more thoroughly.

In leather, though, I omit the basting and just "rub press" the edges all along its length between thumbs and fingers. This gets it pretty much in position before pressing and topstitching.

To get a really straight stitching line in such a prominent place resist the temptation to look at the needle. Concentrate instead on the edge of the presser foot and its proximity to the garment edge. Usually I stitch one line the foot's width from the edge of the garment, second line about $\frac{1}{16}$" from the edge. On this jacket however, I stitched one line 1" from the edge, the second $\frac{3}{8}$" from that. Because it is a large collar, this seemed to look right.

Belts are another way to make the garment unique. To determine the length, tie a tape measure (60") around your waist and decide how much longer or shorter it will be, depending on how it will be buckled or tied. If it needs to be pieced it will look better, smoother if the joining is at an angle.

The belts are stitched wrong side out after interfacing is fused, then turned right side out. Press and topstitch. This is for flat belts. On the red jacket I made a round belt. No interfacing involved, it was stitched then turned right side out over a cable cord which remains as its center core. The end of the cord is left bare for the length of the belt. On the extended cord supply, fold the fabric over it, wrong side out. Stitch that end *across* the fabric through cord and all, and down the fabric length. Turn the fabric over the cord making sure the seam allowances are folded open. After turning, cut off excess cable cord.

That big leather tassel on the end is a piece of leather **3" x 5"**. Slash all along at close intervals in straight lines leaving the top inch intact. Wrap this wrong side out around the belt ends. Stitch or bartack through all layers. Peel it right side out over your stitching and the belt end. It hangs nicely, no stitches showing.

The belt carriers can also be interesting, or unusual, or at least easy to make. On a leather jacket from series 4 there is a casing, then the top of frontier pockets act as the carriers.

On the plum jacket the carriers start as rectangles an inch or so longer than the belt width. Fuse some Wonder Under to its back side, peel off the paper. While warm fold the sides to the center and finger press. It will hold flat. Fold again, press and topstitch edges. Stitch on the garment.

The red jacket with its long tasseled belt needed a softer look. Think of tortellini – those cute little pasta bites. That same shape would make a pretty succession of little loops all around the jacket waistline. These are little rectangles of fabric stitched and turned right side out, pressed only slightly. Stitch them all in place on the jacket on one end. Loop the other end around to overlap and bartack at each edge. At the waist center back I also bartacked the belt so it will always tie the same way in front and can't pull out of the loops.

Another pretty little touch is on a black leather motorcycle jacket with crystal zippers on the pocket, the wrists, the diagonal front zipper. These zippers (we carry them in 4 lengths, call to order) are exposed so the crystals show. A window must be made first. One way is to cut a slash plus corner diagonals where the zipper will be stitched.

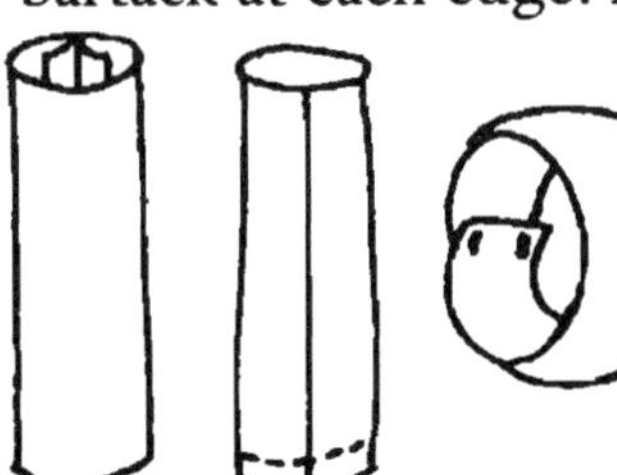

Press back the edges, lay the zipper under the opening. Topstitch in place. The pocket will be positioned and topstitched under it.

If you prefer, cover the intended location with a strip of fusible interfacing, fusible side up. Stitch, slash, turn to the backside and press so everything is secure before stitching in the zipper.

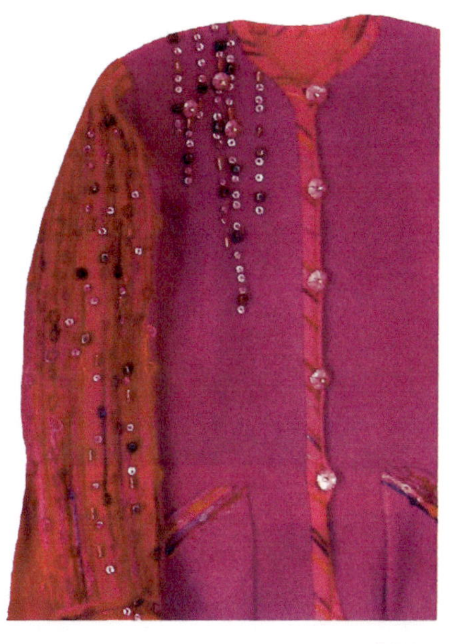

1701 Boiled wool, unappetizing? Not a chance!

1702 Princess lines produce curved seams for a better fit

1702 more Princess Lines . . . .

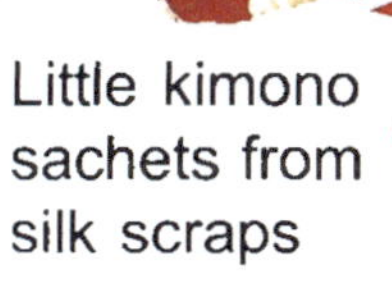

Little kimono sachets from silk scraps

1704 Parade of people with umbrellas walking up a curvy path

1703 Imported Japanese silk in narrow width from Kasuri Dyeworks in Berkley, CA. Candidate for an origami top

• • • Neckline and front cut open, lined, bound for a jacket

1703 Origami folded fabric stitched into place • • •

1705 Three-layer reversible skirt (instructions in Series book 15)

1705 Sheer fabric one layer in a blouse, quilted layers in a vest

1706 Faux leathers tailor well into jacket. Add embellishment by trapunto padding a design

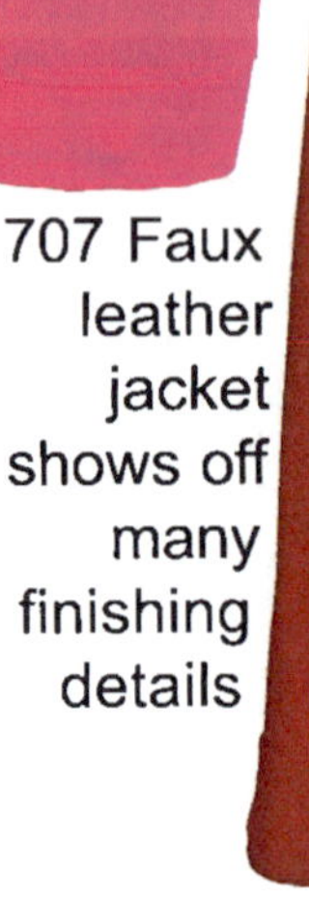

1707 Lacing in and out a row of topstitching

1707 Faux leather jacket shows off many finishing details

1707 Black leather and crystal zippers

1707 Stacked leather cutwork after automatic machine quilted design

1708 ColorBlocking is a great way to make something wearable from odds and ends

1709 Gather together all the treasures of one color, then let them tell you what they will become

1709 What begins as fish skins . . .

. . . is now the lovely textured leather on this bag flap

1708 A silk suit in each of these colors, the vest goes with all of them - colorblocking methods, too

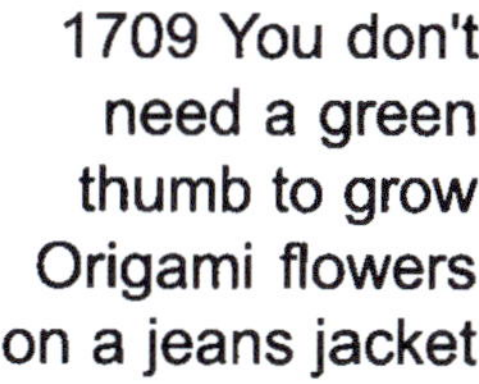

1709 You don't need a green thumb to grow Origami flowers on a jeans jacket

33

1709 From bits and pieces, little assorted treasures, come these bags

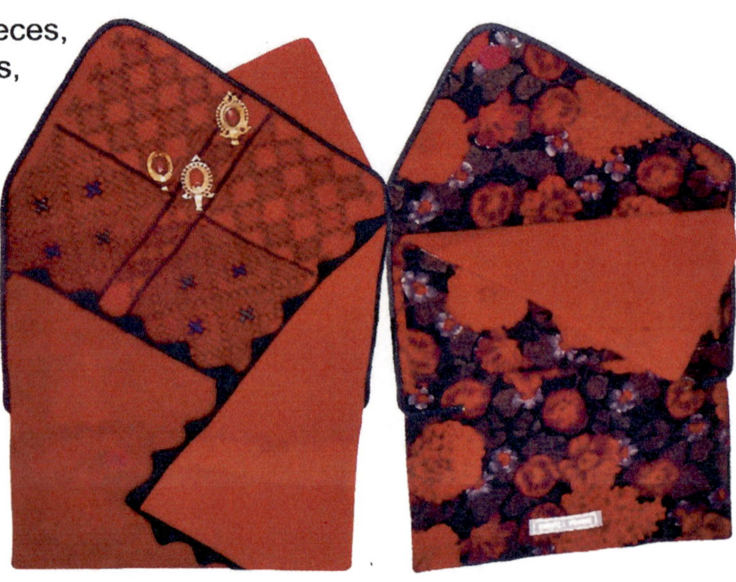

1709 Outside of a bag, and its inside before joining and completing

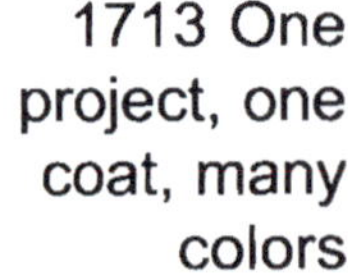

1710 The eyes have it! Less dominant when used upside down

1709 Seminole piecing builds and builds and will then be cut into a garment

1710 Targeted for wearability when simply treated

1713 One project, one coat, many colors

1711 Pull out yarns, insert ribbons, cords, lace, any stripe that strikes your fancy

1712 Squares of crinkle fabric (or ribbon) fan out into flowers

1711 Spinning a yarn to tie colors together

1711 Coats and Clark Stripe thread shows its true colors

1711 The Miracle Stitcher unites the fabrics with yarn application

1712 Projects made from the accent fabric

Inserting these crystal zippers is quite easy since they will be exposed and completely in the open so the crystals show. Just steam press a nice crease in your fabric and pin the fold edge up close to the rows of teeth in the zipper.

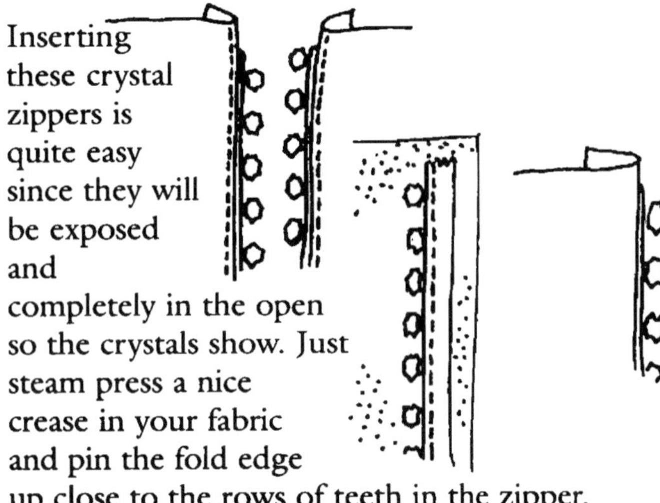

If you do not want stitches showing stitch with zipper back side up, fabric right side against zipper front. When it opens up only the crystal teeth extend beyond the fabric fold back, no stitches showing.

If you need to shorten the zipper, carefully with pliers pull off unwanted top teeth until it is of the correct length. Pull the long zip tape over to the side to stitch zipper in place, then trim off unwanted bare tape.

backside

At the lower end of separating zippers is a plastic protector. You stitch right through that, but use a strong needle (a jeans needle). If you feel better proceeding cautiously, turn the balance wheel by hand those last few stitches.

Lacing is an interesting technique on these leathers. You could use leather narrow strips to lace into polar fleece or other fabrics. The typical way to lace is punching holes with a tool such as a gripper or snap setter. Located $\frac{1}{4}$" to $\frac{1}{2}$" from the garment edge and about $\frac{1}{2}$" apart. The leather lace would be $\frac{1}{4}$" or less wide. The lacing can be done with a tapestry needle or, if you cut the lace tip at an angle, it can be laced without a tool. An easy job, the double layer of the garment is sometimes seamed in attaching the facing. Other times the raw edges are fused together before the eyelets are cut and the lacing is done.

Another possibility once the perforations are cut, just lace in and out like big hand stitches. This is especially true if the trim borders a seam either on a shoulder yoke or in the hip area.

Without perforating the leather, another way to lace is to begin with a row of topstitching. These stitches need to be as long as your lacing is wide. On a red vest my stitches around the neck are about **4.5** in length. These could be laced under rolling round and round but all on the garment outside surface, just going under and held in place by the thread of the topstitching.

Another effect, and the one I chose to do is not going around the thread so the thread itself is concealed. This instead leaves all the thread showing and just goes back and forth under each stitch. At every inside turn it forms an interesting little peak. This is done with a tapestry needle by hand after the stitching on machine is finished. Be sure as you're lacing to keep the leather side up with each stitch. This technique works well with narrow ribbons, braids or tiny bias cut fabric tubes.

More lacing ties the buttons in place. The lace is bartacked to the garment in a suitable location, ends long enough to work with and cut to a slanted point. If the commercial button has large enough holes, lace the leather ends through the button and tie a knot.

A decorative design is quilted on a plum leather vest. Janome's **106** memory card was used for this and it has a huge variety of quilted designs from which to choose. Somewhat like a vine with flower buds on it, it encircles all the vest outer edges. This fabric is backed by fleece, flannel or just a woven cotton before clamping in the machine hoop. Attach the hoop to the machine, push the start button and it quickly stitches the outline you choose. Here's an example of another design on that card. An interesting twist after the stitching is complete is to turn the quilted fabric over so the backside is on top. Carefully cut a little slit in each quilted shape. Push fiberfill into that little slit until the section is stuffed into a third dimension. This really is attractive. The process is called trapunto.

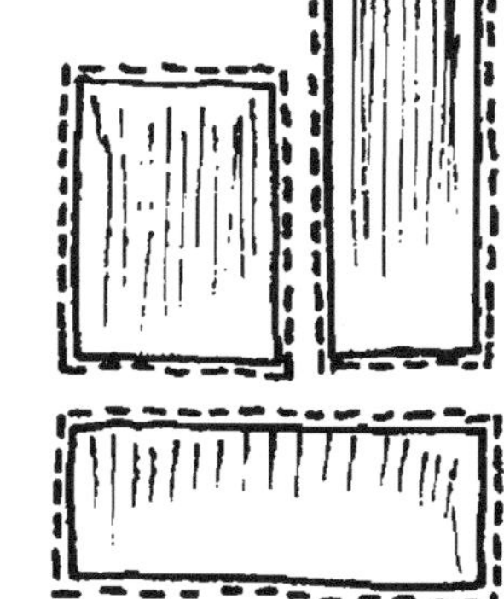

Another alternative is to put 2 or 3 layers together in the hoop and do the automatic quilting. Then cut out some of those sections. The colors of the under layers would then show on the outside. To do this type cutwork in woven fabric would then require a satin stitch covering each raw edge. Because the leather does not ravel, the edge can be left bare, merely cut out. If you haven't this magnificent Janome Memorycraft 9000 something similar can still be done freehand. Draw or trace a design on the surface and then stitch around it. Or rather than drawing, cut out shapes in computer labels or post-it notes. Stick them on the fabric surface and stitch around them. They can be reused many times and pins wouldn't be needed.

Any of these embellishment type products are thoroughly enjoyable. I love the end results, but the fun is in the doing! Great hobby, sewing.

Faux Leathers courtesy of
Donna Salyers Fabulous Furs
25 West Robbins Street
Covington, KY 41011
www.fabulousfurs.com
1-800-848-4650

ColorBlocking Chapter 8

A lot of you sewers are also quilters, and all those little pieces you join together could be considered colorblocking. But usually colors are in bigger blocks and you may have different reasons for putting them together. I have three different outfits in silk suiting in deep jewel colors and when there's a scrap of each left over, lets rerun them into something new.

Colorblocking continues to be popular year after year and is a marvelous way to:

- Pad out, supplementing when you run short of a fabric.

- Use up leftovers of this and that making a new item to coordinate garments already in the closet

- Add-on width or length to an existing item whose size you want to increase

- As a bridge tying together this blouse and that skirt into a coordinated outfit

From several other projects, all made from thin or sheer fabrics in blue and green tints and shades I had many scraps. Alone none of these could make anything but a little teamwork goes a long way. By combining them all to color block, a blouse or some other garment can result. In colorblocking the decision initially is usually whether to cut up a duplicate pattern adding seams to each cut edge – or – first seam together many fabrics to build a large fabric. Then lay your pattern and cut out.

The vest from heavy silk suiting remnants was best cut up at the pattern stage as it had larger pieces with curved edges. Small pieces like those in my

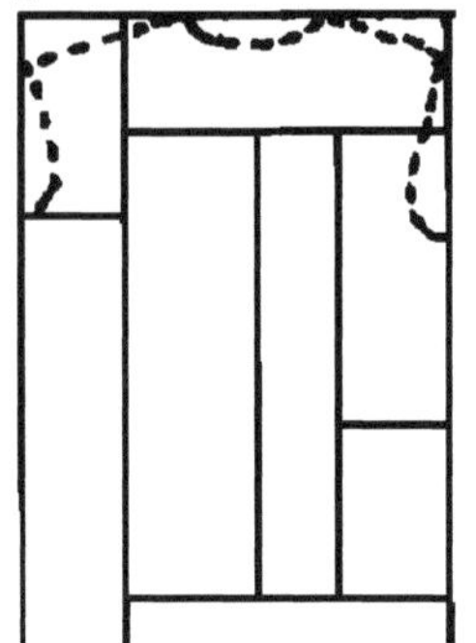

log cabin blouse are best done first building the fabric, cutting blouse shapes later. I really don't want to build a huge piece of fabric and lay all patten pieces on it. Rather, I would

build each log cabin just large enough for one pattern piece, build another for the next, and so on until all pattern pieces have fabric.

If this log cabin is designated for a more structured garment like a jacket I seam it all on the sewing machine, pressing seams to one side after each joining. This is because interfacing or batting and lining will back it. The blouse will have no backing so all seams on this sheer, ravelly fabric must be finished. A serger works well for the fabric construction. If the fabric is opaque, a **4**-thread overlock stitch is best to both have one needle thread for the sturdy seam, other threads for binding the raw edges. For transparent fabric, a rolled hem edge produces a tiny seam less then $\frac{1}{8}$" wide that looks nice as you see through the fabric. Because the fabric actually rolls over in the process, there is more enclosed fabric than appears so it is strong enough to not pull apart. Use this method to set in sleeves in a chiffon or organza top. Only a heavy pencil line shows, not an actual seam allowance.

To make a pattern for a vest or other garment with curved lines, start with a duplicate paper pattern since you will cut it up. Draw lines on it where you want to cut the divisions apart. On a garment that will button, make the divisions right there to incorporate in-seam buttonholes. Draw grainlines before cutting apart.

Vertical dart – fold it out for a better design. The fit will be the same as if you had a stitched dart. Notice how a little jut forms at the dart folds. Simply smooth out as you add seams. Tape seams on if you feel the need. I will just lay these pattern pieces on my various pieces of fabric observing the straight grain. Chalk or pin a reminder of the seams to be added on the fabric itself.

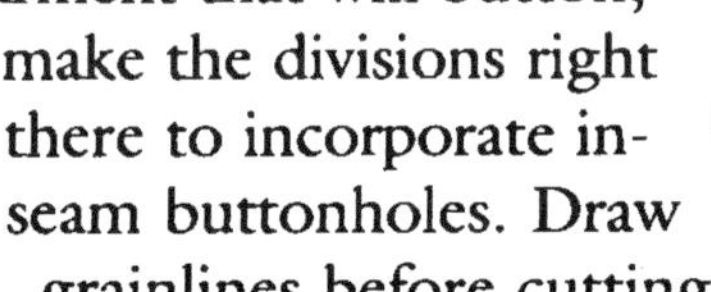

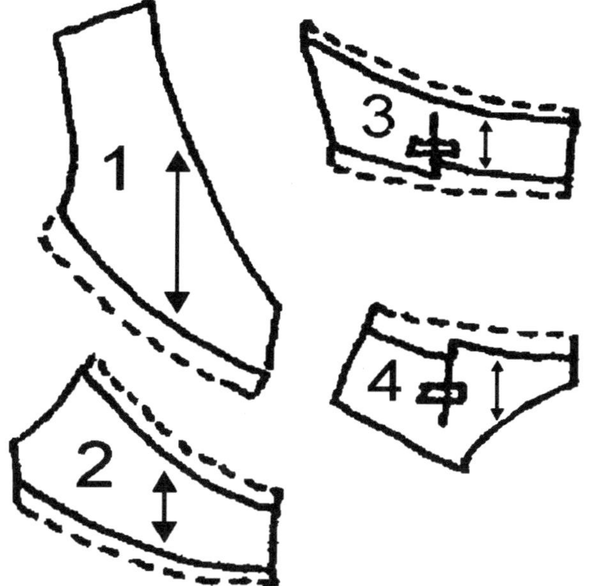

In ColorBlocking, horizontal seams pose no problems matching up. If however, you opted for a curved or diagonal shaping, the fabric edge **beyond** the center front will need to match.

When this vest is buttoned you can see how they don't come out just right. If however, the vest is worn open they would look just fine and the joining levels would be the same at the edges. This may be completely insignificant to some. If it matters to you think about it in advance and set the left side down a little lower to compensate.

These broad, horizontally seamed places are ideal for inseam buttonholes. They are wonderful in that they're invisible. When the garment hangs open there is no hint of a buttonhole and maybe with the colorblocking enough is going on; buttonholes would only clutter the whole design.

To construct these, measure the button to determine exactly how large the opening needs to be. Remember to add its thickness to the button diameter. To be sure, take the button to your closet and find just the right size for it to button through.

Stitch the seam joining the two pieces of fabric, after marking where the opening should be. Buttonholes ordinarily start $1/8$" to the left of the center front to allow space for the button shank. They extend out to the right as far as is necessary to accommodate the button. Stitch the seam up to the buttonhole end and backstitch. Do the same for the short distance from the other end to the front edge. You have left an opening of the proper size. Press the seam open.

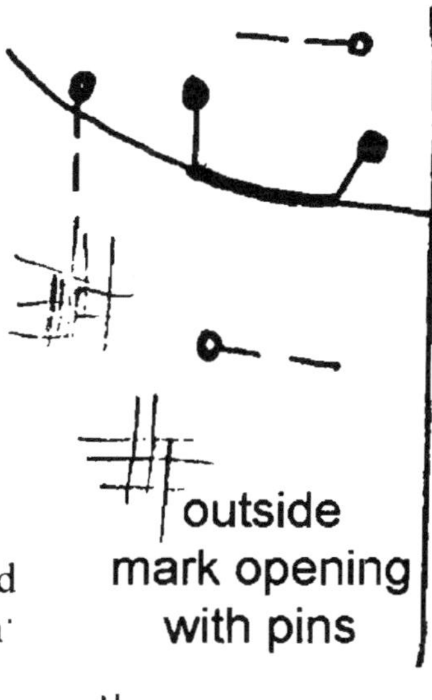

Buttonhole is complete when the facing or lining, whichever covers the back, is slashed open and stitched in place. Pin this back layer to the garment around the buttonhole area so both layers are secured flatly in place. At each end of the opening, stab a pin through to mark the position of the facing side. Slash a line between the two pins being careful to not penetrate the outer garment. If this fabric is at all ravelly fuse a strip of sheer tricot interfacing to it before sewing into the garment so this cut edge won't fall apart

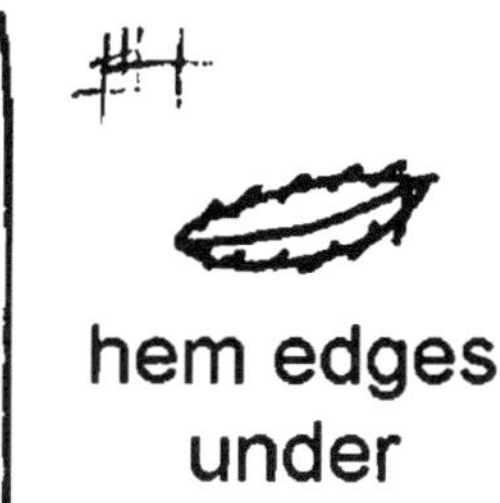

before you can get it hand stitched. Fold under the facing edges into an elliptical shape and whip the folded edge down by hand in little invisible stitches to the seam allowances of the outer fabric.

Sewing an inside-outside curve together, even if only a shallow gentle curve, will necessitate clipping the *inside* curve. To pin and stitch the edges together then works well since the inside curve will open up straight to conform to the

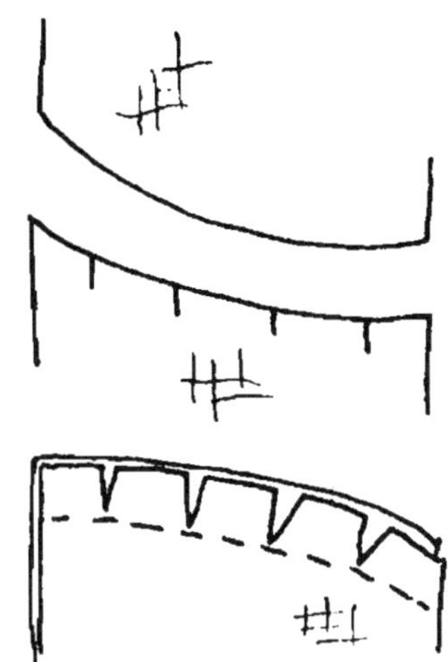

shape of the outside curve. When that seam is pressed open the clips will pull open slightly, looking like notches, because that fabric edge is folded back into a larger area. The opposite happens in the outside curved edge. It probably won't need clipping before stitching together but in pressing, if the excess fullness of the edge won't press flat, notches may have to be cut in it to have a

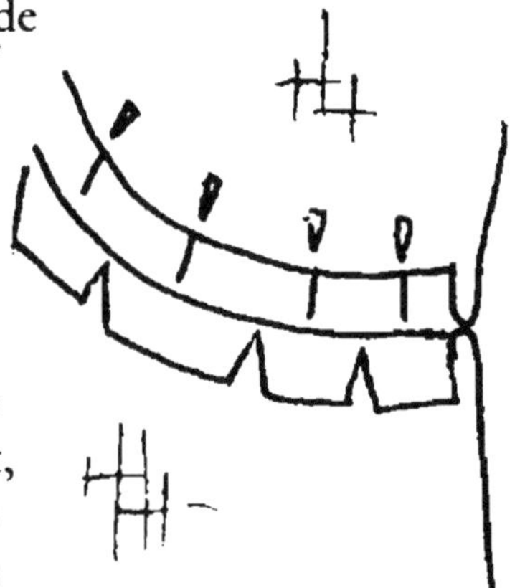

smooth outward appearance. If seams will be trimmed off shorter this may be unnecessary.

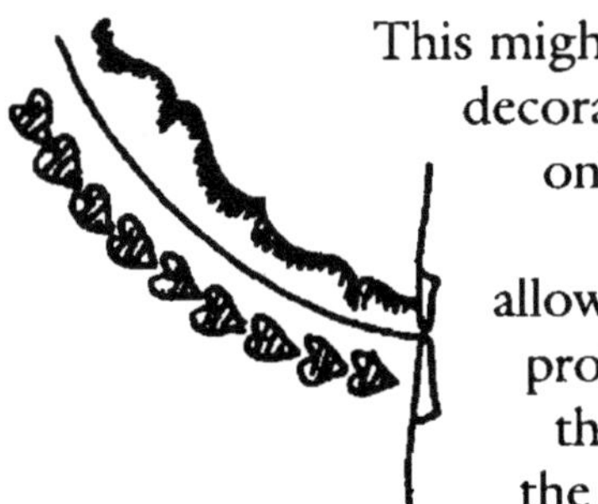

This might be a good place for decorative topstitching not only pretty, but to hold down the seam allowances. Your machine probably has a variety of these and this could be the perfect accent in just the right color threads.

Joining an inside-outside corner needs special treatment. Reinforce the inside corner with small stitches slanted slightly into the seam allowance on each side. Clip to the corner where

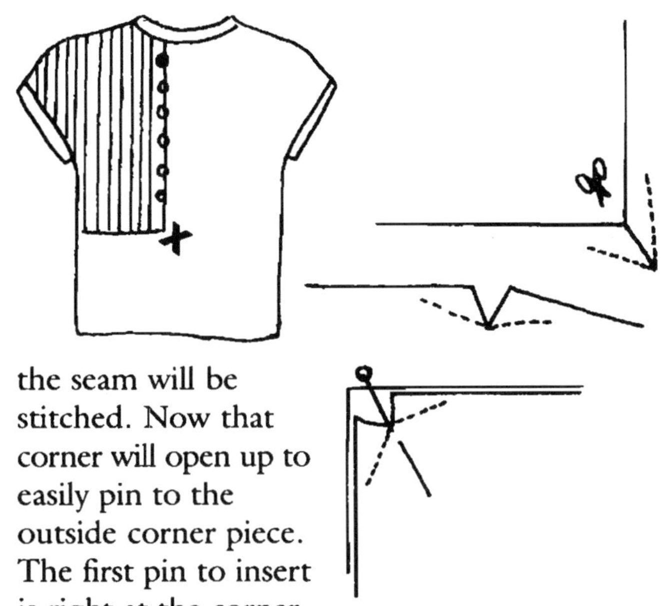

the seam will be stitched. Now that corner will open up to easily pin to the outside corner piece. The first pin to insert is right at the corner, pulling the cut up high enough to form a perfect square. Then put in the surrounding pins and stitch. The stitches should be smaller surrounding the corner for greater security at this potentially endangered spot.

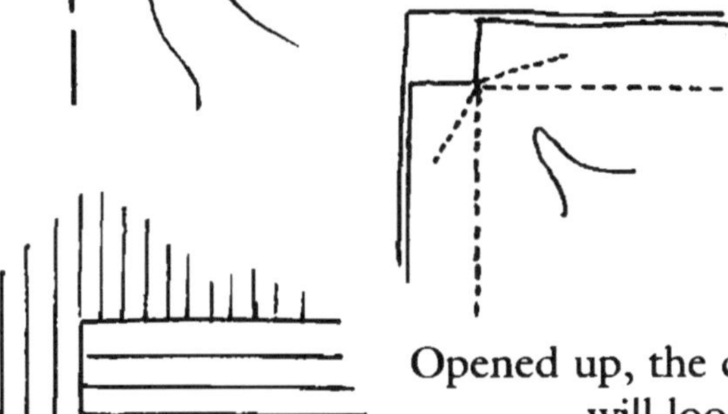

Opened up, the corner will look very professional. If that initial pin allows the slashed corner to be lazy and droop down a little lower as it is stitched, the results will be more rounded and rather disappointing.

Other color blocking might be in stripes, vertical or horizontal. If you make these uneven in width, they can be even more interesting. Mix some prints in with solids as long as they have a unifying quality – usually color. Examples are at the top of the next page.

Think of doing this as a lining to put a little fun in your wardrobe. Currently I'm planning a denim coat in just a plain usual dark blue with probably some interesting textural features such as pintucks, couched yarns and threads, groups of buttons or beads. But all in the same blue, the surface embellishment won't show all that much except at close range.

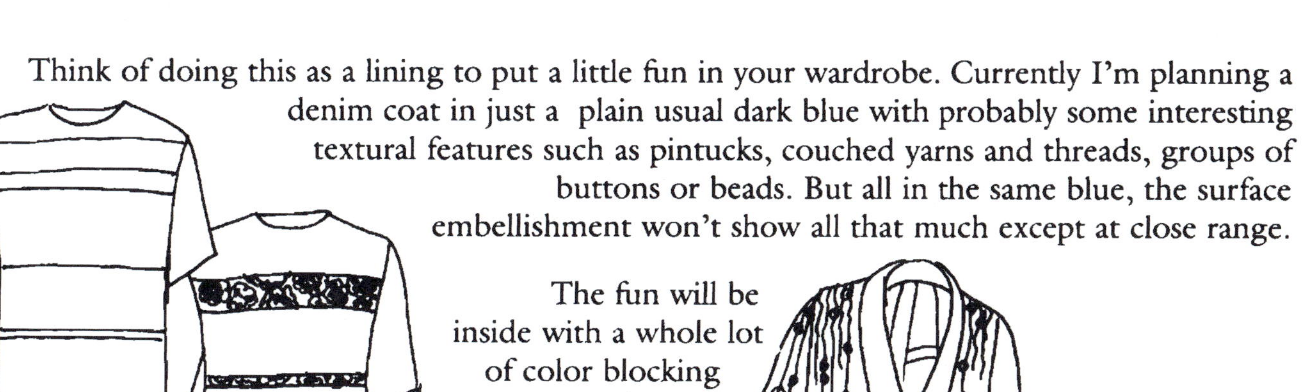

The fun will be inside with a whole lot of color blocking uniting a large number of cotton prints. Fat quarter cuts in a quilt shop are usually displayed all color grouped making it very easy to combine a coordinated melange.

A shirt I'm making has a Mondrian quality as I first laid black twill tape strips in wide bold widths over its surface. Then patches of multi-colored fabrics are laid here and there, raw edges slid under existing tapes before pinning everything down. Narrow tapes cover the remaining raw fabric edges and everything is stitched in place permanently. No talent required, everyone can do these things and quite enjoyably, too!

Piet Mondrian is the artist whose work looks like this

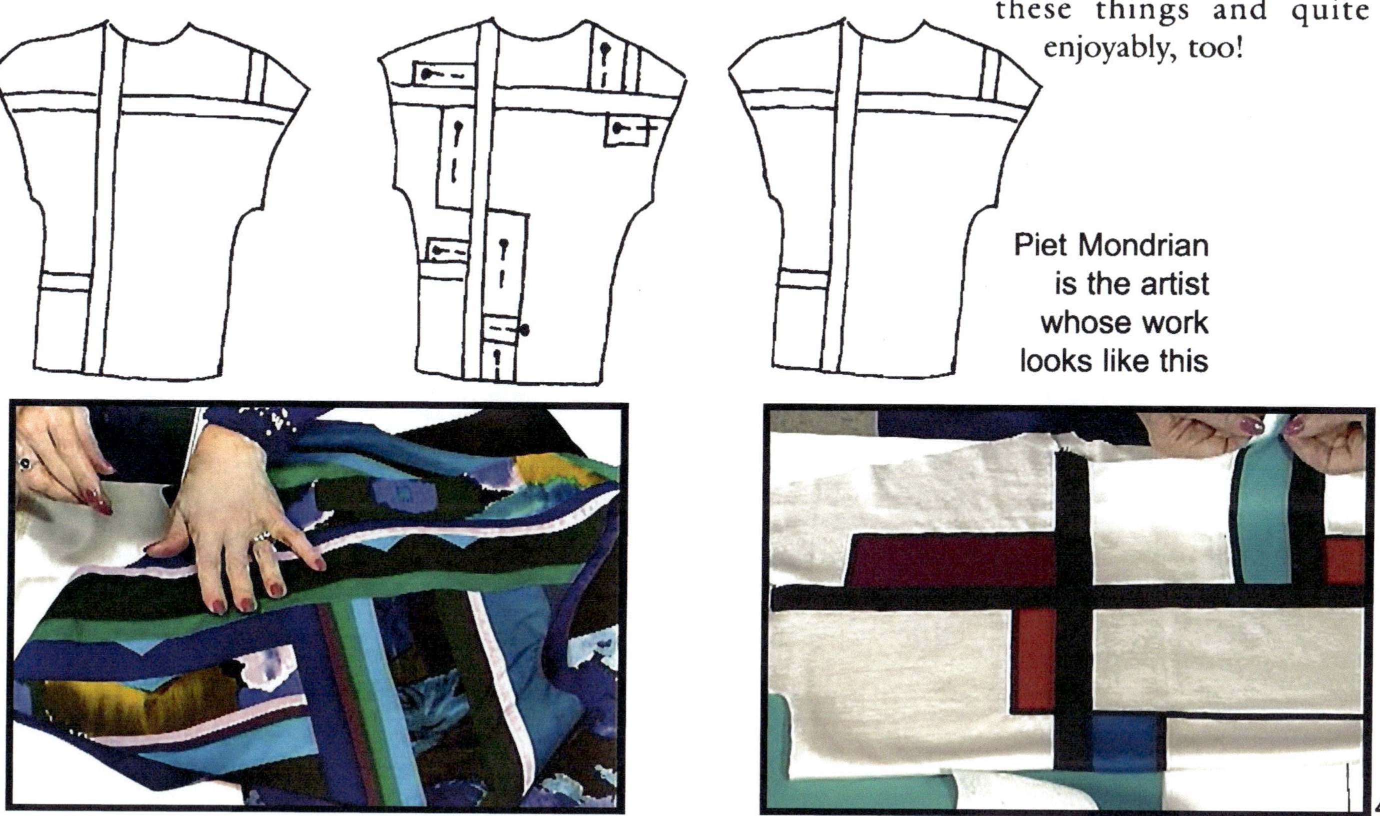

Collecting Color

In live seminars I'm always asked questions concerning putting it all together. How do you decide what fabrics you can combine for a project? What notions, trims and embellishments will make it look complete, unique, elegant?

For me it all starts out with big zip lock bags. Collect in them groups of things that look like they belong together. Simple as that, when you come across another likely candidate, put it in the bag. Add some magazine clippings. Before long it becomes obvious that some things don't quite click so you take them out and redirect down another path.

The cement that holds all these separate components together is *color*. What eliminates some of the elements in the bag? Maybe a contradiction in moods such as earthy *vs* glitzy. Fabrics and trims that have different care requirements like dry clean only *vs* wash only. Prints may have identical colors, but look terrible mixed together. Collect them all first, then break them all down into perfect combinations just meant for each other.

Plums

One grouping is in plums, purples, magentas, pinks. They all went in one bag because of the color, but some are more subdued, others brighter. I love the interplay of textures between the leathers, suedes, print cotton, print silk, rough tweed, but obviously they can't all go together. Some of them start asking for a little distance please! In this bag is also a handful of distinctive buttons and as I try each on one fabric, then another, preferences begin to jump forward.

Plum Garment #1

A heavy print cotton (used in the jacket on the cover of The Sewing Connection Series 6) has a particular affinity for a deep plum leather from the jacket in chapter 1706.

A lovely button in a dull matte plum is the identical color as found in the print and it has deeply grooved series of curvy line in high and low relief. It suggests to me quilting the print fabric into a vest perhaps using heavy cords or yarns to do the quilting by couching them over the surface.

In the next flash that button says no, think instead of quilting with the right side of the fabric down, batting on top and winding a novelty thread on the bobbin to stitch rather than couch the quilted lines. The scrap plum leather volunteers to band the vest edges and it would be a great coordinate with the 1706 jacket.

Magenta Project #2

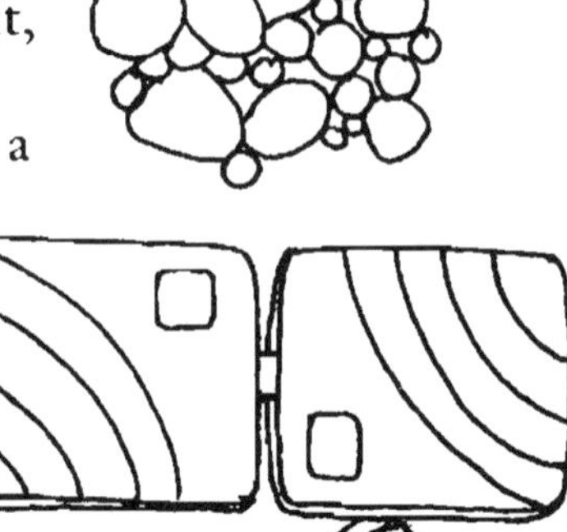

Three different magenta suedes are the identical color but one is solid, the other a herringbone design embossed on it, the third is rounded embossed shapes like a whole pebbled surface. A two-piece buckle that came off a favorite old worn-out belt is in the same color.

A magazine clipping in the bag shows a pair of very expensive shoes in pintucked suede in three different colors. These components suddenly click into the finished piece! They will be a shoulder bag cut from the series 9 Bucket Bag pattern stitched together in wavy sections.

Are you starting to see what I mean when I keep advising "Let your fabric speak". It really does begin to make beautifully logical sense and this combining of elements is such fun, I could spend

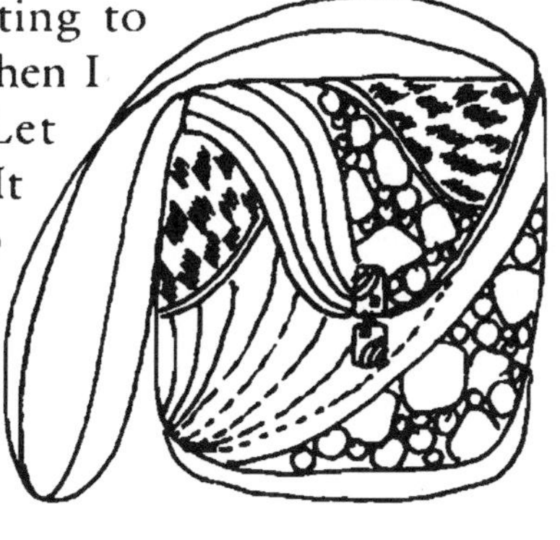

endless time entertaining myself with the pairing and matching.

Another little double clutch bag I've already made from these same magenta suedes in series 15.

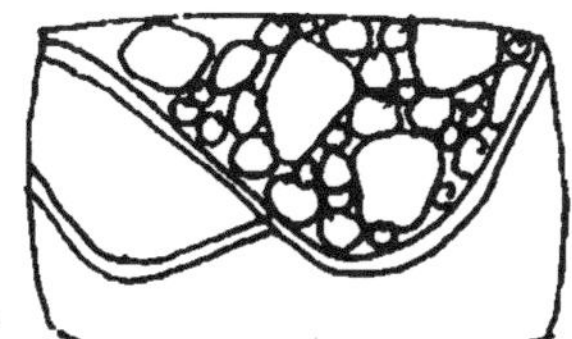

Still another suede is a subdued amethyst color. There's a matte button which is a perfect match and my head says go with this, adding to it a wool flannel coordinate. I have another button that speaks on a different level. It is sort of circular, but a little irregular in shape. Its surface is slightly indented inviting your thumb to rub over it soothingly. A rich inner glow comes from its

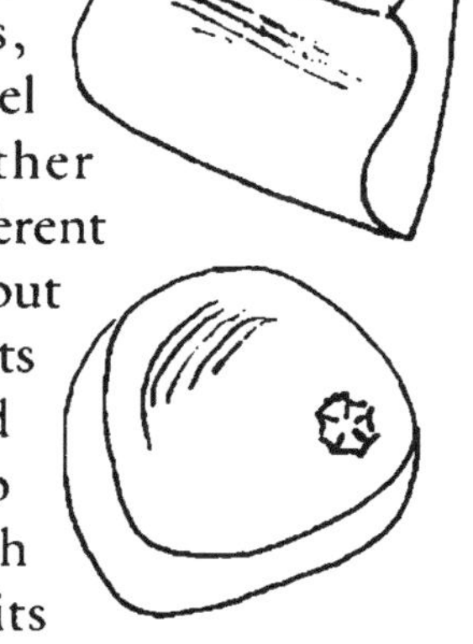

depth and a crystal near the edge twinkles. The color is perfect for the suede, but suede with a gem in its button? Completely illogical. To look at it on the suede makes my heart beat a little faster. The jury is still out on that one so they will remain in a zip-lock for a later decision.

Completely discarded from this group is a piece of too bright pink that goes with nothing here because of the startling intensity. Also discarded is a great button which looks like a chunk of pink ice or the sparkly but uncut surface of a gem in the rough. These two will be put back in drawers to await a project another time.

Olives Project #1

Another big bag is a treasury of olive fabrics. From this a silk blouse is made for Chapter 11 along with a couple of buttons, perfect for it. Since only two buttons were

available the styling takes shape. Put them on a large collar up high where they show. Use concealed buttons and buttonholes down the front in a clear plastic since they won't be seen. Make slim

long sleeves requiring no buttons at the wrist.

Project #2

A print in stripes is an unusual color combination in olive, magenta and purple. Use magenta piping at the armscye seams around the neck and down the fronts. It will go beautifully with

the bag from the previous magenta group and a skirt I have made from the same suede. The purple in the print is a perfect match to the 1706 leather jacket. That jacket is really dark and this gives it a breath of lively freshness. I love prints that will go several directions making them versatile wardrobe additions. Come to think of it, I have a really dull green suit which is a perfect complement. What a great find!

Project #3

An olive silk shantung doesn't quite go with any of the other fabrics, but in that bag are

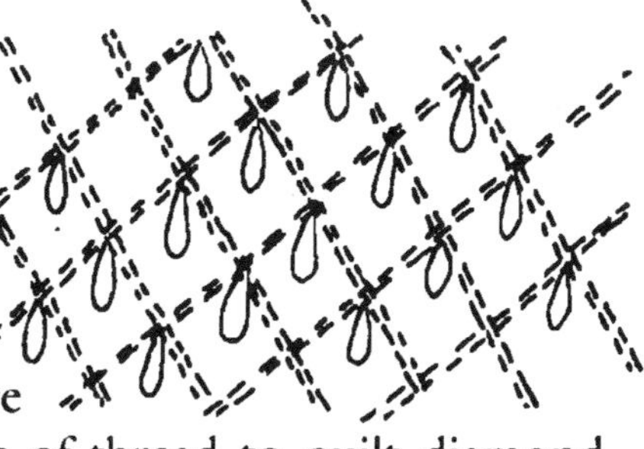

all sorts of spools of thread to quilt diamond shaped lines. Also in the bag are buttons and beads. Use little beads the size of watermelon seeds, but in olive, sewn at every crossing. There are a whole collection of yarns, very textury, varying thicknesses. Wouldn't it be fun to use a Miracle Stitcher, that Janome attachment I love that enables you to couch in any direction, and quilt a vest with these beauties! A grouping of beads that look like tney green pumpkins would be fun on this. I think this vest idea just won out, and will be what I make. Some of you like to buy all the components together in kits, but for me, never. Designing I absolutely love to do.

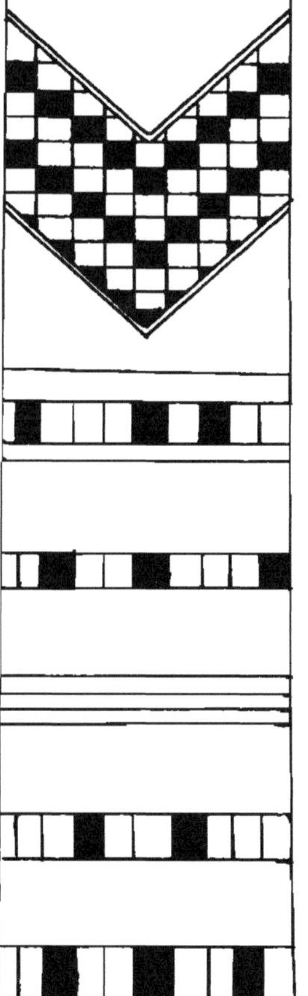

Project #4

In Australia I saw something marvelous. Many restaurants had baramundi on their menu in the seafood area. Then in a quaint little village I saw a woman making doll boots from this great texturey leather. Turns out it was a baramundi skin, scaled, tanned and dyed into a buttery soft leather! Can you imagine? I bought a greenish one on the spot but she sent me another – a story I'll tell you later. This green one is perfect with some pale lime suede and a greenish-gold leather. Picture it in a shoulder bag.

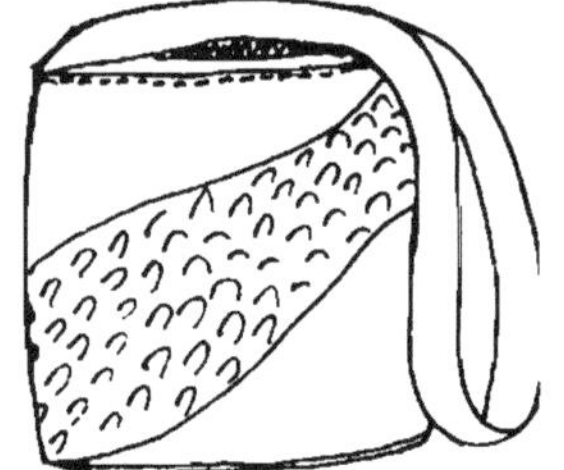
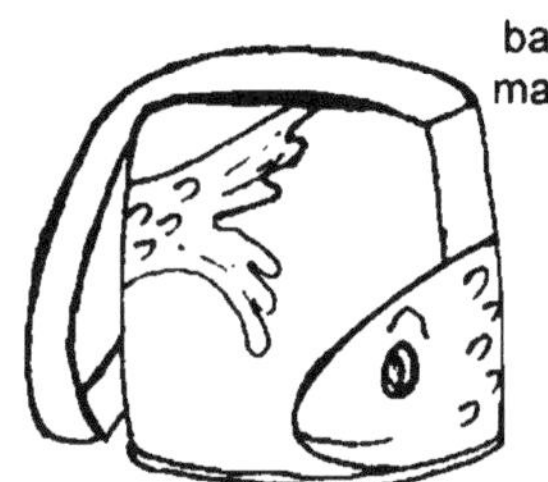

An Oriental print silk rectangle looks so nice with this combination, it will probably become the bag lining. It used to be a Japanese kimono that was taken apart, small pieces sold.

Project #5

The other baramundi skin? Here is it's off-color story. Before you raise eyebrows, it's off-color only because it's not olive. October arrived and this marvelous little package came from Australia – my beautiful- plum charcoal fish skin! I had bought it in April and given up

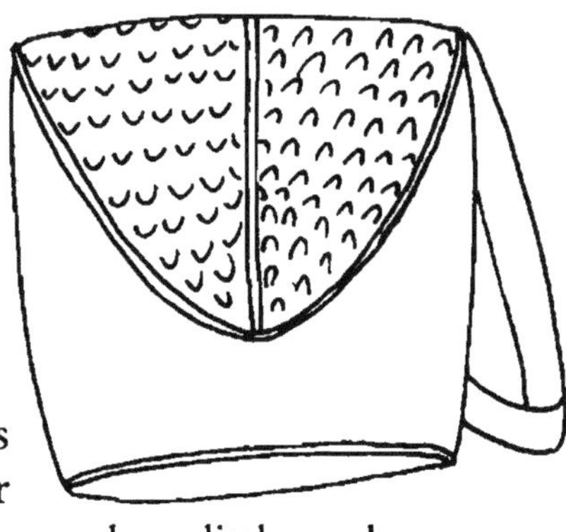

all hope of ever receiving it after 6 months. I looked at the post mark and it had been mailed air express first of May! Where could it possibly have been for one-half year! Is there a hot air balloon slowly floating around the world delivering such mail? Thanks so much to Roz Branson of Hahndorf, the delightful Australian woman who sent it to me. It became a shoulder bag within days of its arrival. The fish skin is the fold down flap, cut in half, a leather piping down the center. In other words half that fish is swimming upstream, half downstream. I really love discovering such unusual raw materials.

As usual, several of my treasures from the olive bag are undesignated, but one day each will be the perfect answer to aproject. At that time I will be delighted I bought it years earlier.

Moving On

In series 15 I showed a vest of Seminole piecing in silk, in gem colors of blues, greens, purples. This started out by sewing many narrow strips together and pressing seams to one side. These are then cut crosswise and stitched together again offsetting each color by one square. After showing the technique and then having a lot of the original pieced section left over, it seems wasteful of time and effort to not use this for some good purpose. That purpose is not an absolute at this point. It will be a vest or a jacket and maybe a purse. Meanwhile I've stitched a piping at each end of the seminole V and keep adding on to it. Solid strips of purple silk are of variable lengths for a more interesting overall picture. There are intermittent strips of the pieced fabric, some lengthwise and some crosswise. So far I have about a 6' strip of this which will then be cut up to make whatever project it seems to want to be.

From India I have an embroidered piece about 6" square mostly in reds with touches of forest green. In my scrap collection, pieces of UltraSuede from deep red to orange-red perfectly blend with the embroidery colors. They fit on the basic purse background surrounding the embroidered piece. Some large green rickrack surrounds and accents the embroidery. Turn over and trim off the excess suede beyond the shaped fusible fleece purse form edge.

Just briefly, all these little purses are made by the same formula. The fusible fleece shape is cut out from the pattern (Clutch Bag Pattern) and fused to the fashion fabric. Embellish it as you please. Fuse a rectangle of fusible interfacing unto lining fabric, the size a little larger than the pattern. Right sides together, sew all around near the fleece edge, leaving an opening on the top flat edge for turning.

With pinking shears cut off all around the edge. Turn right side out and press very flat. Zigzag the opening together with monofilament thread both in the needle and the bobbin. From the fold line near the flat edge, around the curved part to the other fold line, zigzag a cord edging onto the bag edge. Fold up the bottom one-third and zigzag the sides in place. Attach a fastener of snaps or Velcro. More complete directions can be found in The Clutch Bag pattern as well as explicit ideas for several more styles. Books 5, 8, 9, 10, 12 and 14 have other handbag ideas and specifics if you find this an intriguing way to create pretty things from bits and pieces.

Ann Wall of Texas makes UltraSuede cutwork patterns. She gave me a 4" square sample of her work in red and black. Using my clutch bag pattern with the rounded flap, I cut it as a point. The pretty sample is turned on point and matches the bag edge as it is appliquéed on plain black UltraSuede to enlarge it for a neat little purse. Enlarged precious treasures you have could go into some wonderful project.

Origami Hydrangea

Inspired by Kumiko Sudo
Fabled Flowers

sewingconnection.com/hydrangea

Cotton fat quarters form the petals; busy patterned taffeta possessed the perfect colors for the leaves. Stitching shows the leaf structure. Bag constructed of heavy denim.

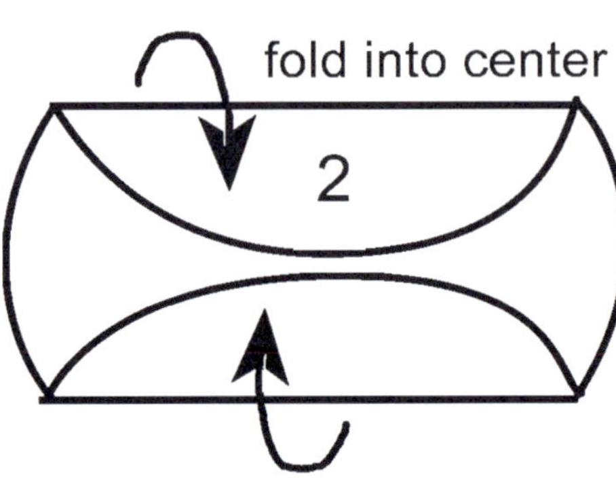

fold into center

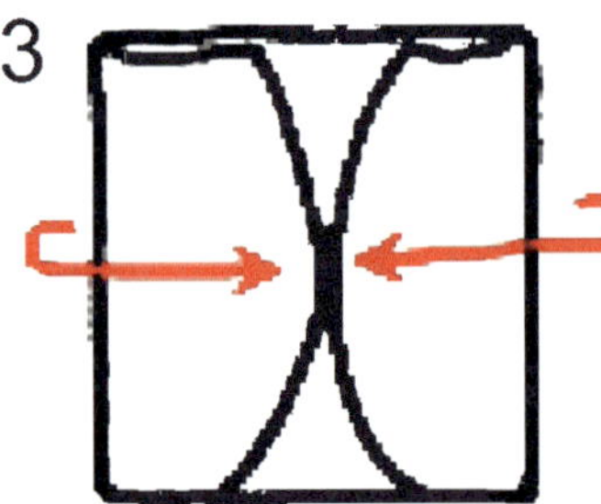

3

fold ends into center
to form a square

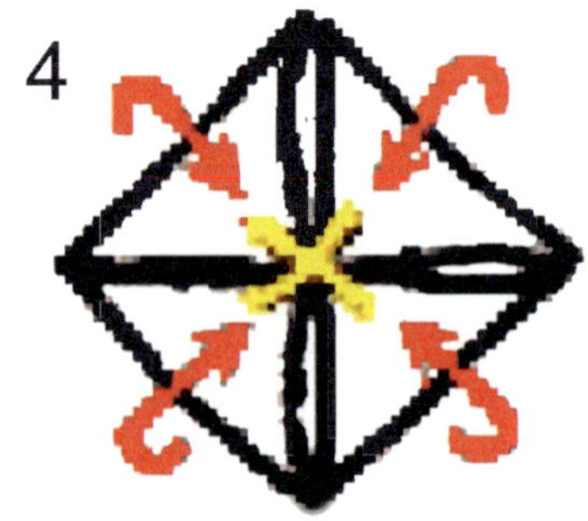

4

fold corners into
center to make diamond
then bartack center
creating an X
which is the eye of the petal

Sometimes I find in my collection some really wild fabrics I can't think why I bought. Judging from your letters I'm not alone as you keep asking me how to handle them, what to do with them. These are big motifs such as scarf panels or other bold isolated designs as opposed to all-over prints.

For starters keep a file. Cut out of catalogs and magazines any ideas that you like which might be used in the future. This shows how others have used such a print in this skirt or that top. You might do something completely different but at least this breaks the ice getting the wheels turning. Think of motif location on your body for the most flattering look. Think how to cut up these specimen fabrics or how to join them together as they always take more decision time than easier fabrics.

One print I have, bought by the panel rather than by the yard, has a big red design in the center, half designs at each selvage edge, on a black background. Think where you would wear this on your body. Wherever it is, it's difficult for anyone talking with you to look you in the eye as those huge owl eyes are staring at you! A rather intense print and maybe hard to live in. Try turning such a print upside down and it tells a completely different story. It looks like African masks perhaps, but easier to look at this way and less compelling.

This came from a manufacturer's outlet, and I don't know what they were making from this – probably blouses. One obvious way to use this is for the center motif to become the blouse back; the side pieces for the blouse front with an overlap;

for buttons and buttonholes. Those side motifs don't stop right at the center, but go three inches beyond, out to the selvege. This extra would allow you to perfectly match the center front, have an extension for buttons and buttonholes, and have a fold-back facing.

It would look best if all motifs are at the same level so remember the plaid and stripe matching technique I've frequently mentioned. Put the pattern's underarm points at the same level and it will come out just right every time. Lay the front pattern piece first, as motif location is most important here, the back and sleeves secondary. Position it so its *center front line* is right on the center line of the selvege motif. The left front does the same over on the left selvage. When later finished and buttoned in place the match will be so perfect it will be difficult to see the break as you'll notice in the red and black photo (centerfold).

The back pattern will then be easy to place on the same level and it will match going across. This project turned into a vest, by the way, and the dotted lines show how it was cut with a high neck and a longer straight lower edge. Ordinarily this type print has enough solid color between

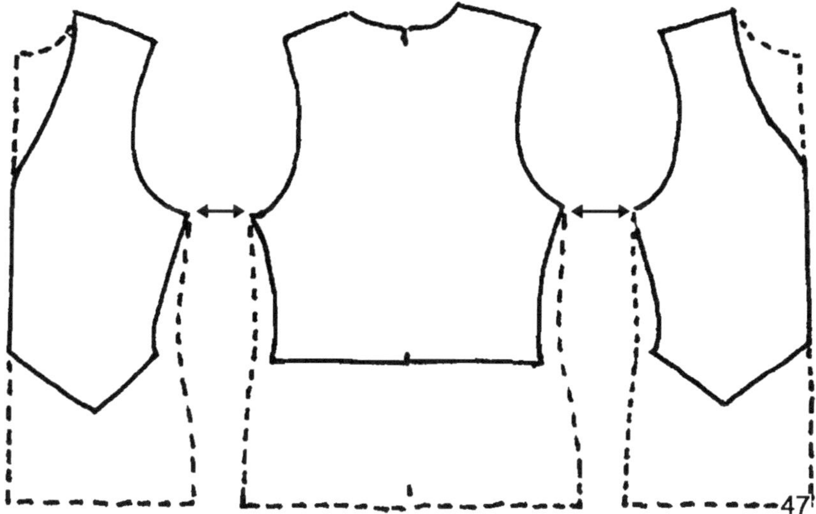

the motifs to allow for larger or smaller bodies wearing it without effecting the design itself. If too narrow in the fabric width even then, add a plain panel at the side to extend.

If a vest, there is a possibility of leaving the side seam open below the waist. It hangs well this way without pulling snugly in the hip area. This vest was made long to have a drawstring at the waist.

Make a buttonhole first in the outer fabric right at the waistline, about 2" from the front edge. Line the vest, hem it, finish all details. The final thing then is stitching two rows anchoring the lining and outer fabric together and producing a casing in the process. Insert the tie belt through a buttonhole pulling through the casing with a bodkin or a large safety pin. Come out at the other end's buttonhole and even it up so the belt's center is at the vest center back. Bartack the center and the belt will never pull out accidentally.

If the fabric print you are using is too overpowering, you might obscure it, making it more interesting in the process. For example, had my red and black print just been more than I cared to face I might have cut several straight black strips from another fabric. Again, to make this more interesting, cut the strips irregular widths. My favorite tool

48

for this is Fiskars Craft Cutter. It is a **24"** acrylic ruler with attached rotary blade. I love this gadget. It has a rubber rim under the cutter edge that holds the fabric firmly so nothing moves. The blades are interchangeable between straight, wave, pinking, etc. Either appliqué these strips over the top or slash the design into irregular strips, and seam together. Use either method to enlarge too narrow fabrics.

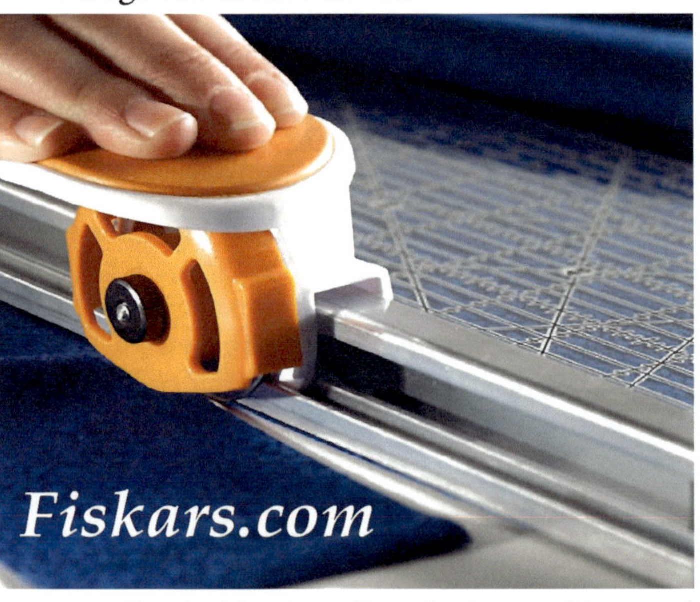

For bold prints, I prefer less architectural structure. For example, a baseball jacket from series 12 is cut with only underarm seams, the whole jacket being one piece except for neck, wrist, and lower

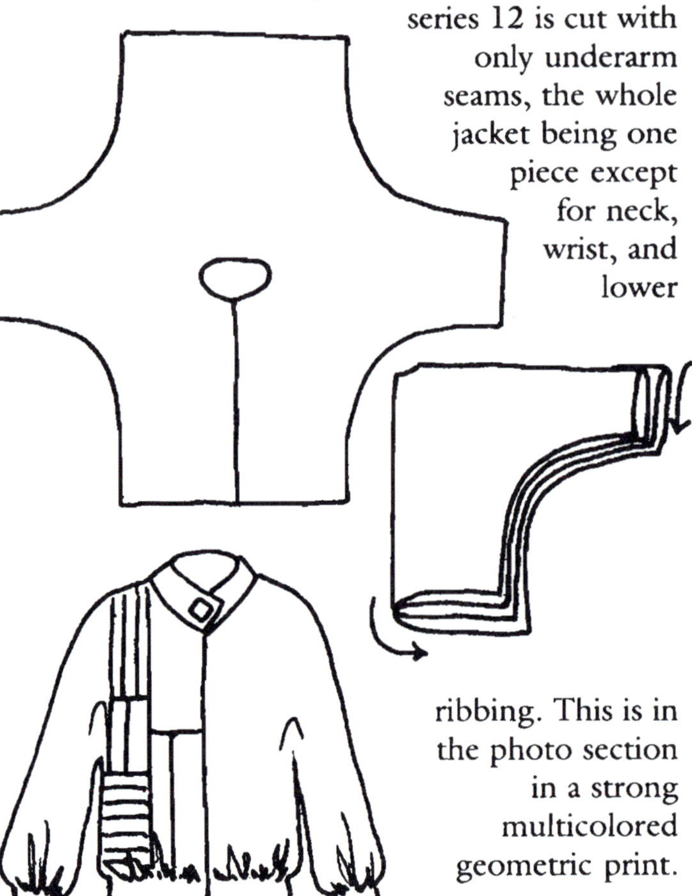

ribbing. This is in the photo section in a strong multicolored geometric print.

Also photographed is a dress with enormous tulips all over. They look fine now, but when first cut out, the location of these tulips on the body wasn't well thought out. Two large flowers appeared on the upper chest. At least they weren't on the bust, up above, but bad enough. The answer is to use a fusible on the back of a tulip leaf and partially cover up one of them.

The jacket I wear on this show is black with big red flowers. Where the one button overlaps it at the waist, this seemed like a good place to center one big flower with the button forming its middle. To cut this so it has a·perfect overlap, cut one front at a time, not double layers. Position that one flower at the waistline so its center is on the marked center front line. After cutting it out clip a little marker with scissors at the center front top and bottom. Remove the pattern. Don't turn over the fabric. Move it on top the uncut fabric and find a spot where its front edge disappears into a perfect match. Tuck a pin in the uncut fabric, top and bottom, right where the little clips are. Remove the cut front. Turn the pattern over because now you need a left front. Place its center front line right between those two pins and cut out. It will be a perfect match.

Bold prints are sometimes more pleasant in small doses. A large animal print silk makes a lovely blouse. I like it best with a plain black skirt or pants rather than using the print over the whole body. To tone it down this way is more wearable, but also delivers more impact.

A scarf square is another type print which requires some thought. One of the prints in my collection was a big circle. I had two of these and treated them very simply, one back and one front creating a simple cap-sleeved shell to wear under a jacket.

Another scarf print with borders is 4 in a piece. I really like the print and the color, but deciding what to do with it is taking a couple of years. I can see it as

a wrap skirt, using only two squares – worn with a black top. It could be a dress centering the four panels as shown (next page), but what to do with the dress back? A jacket is a possibility and this would give enough for back and front, possibly cut like the one-piece jacket in series 12.

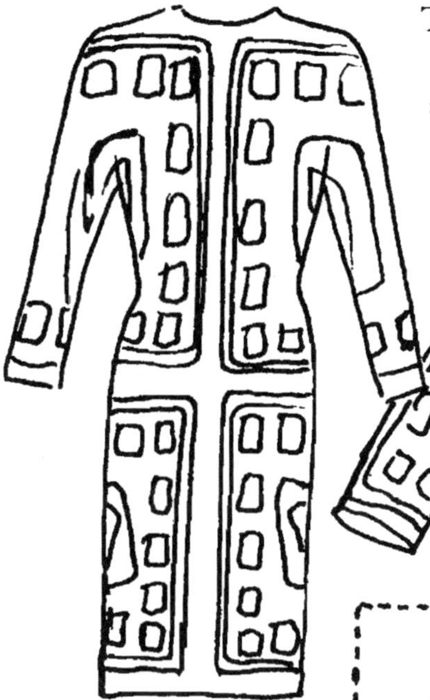

This could be turned on the bias. Before cutting anything though, stand in front of a mirror and see what

happens as an optical illusion. If this is centered so a square is in one location, your body assumes barrel-like dimensions. If you move it another way, it broadens your shoulders and makes your waist look very shapely.

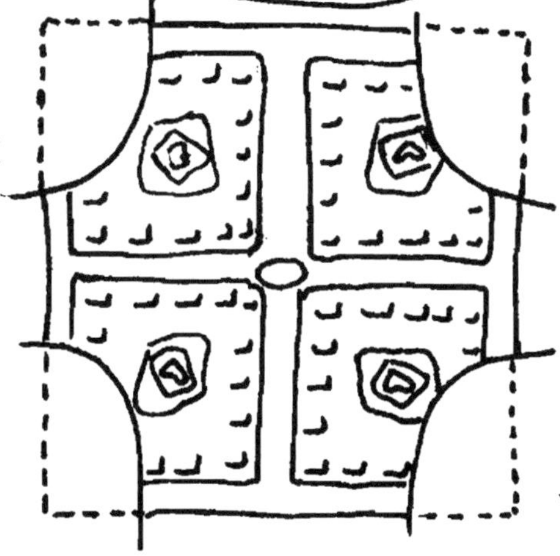

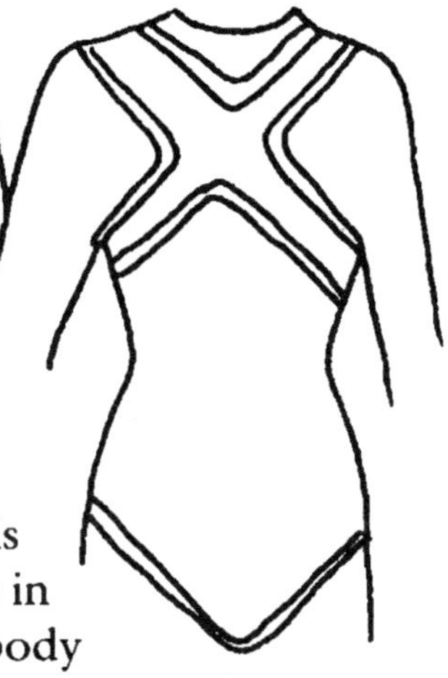

Another possibility is using the borders and filling centers with a plain fabric. Use the centers quilted as patch pockets on a solid color. Maybe use parts of the garment plain, others the print. Alternatives are just endless and a collection of clippings are really wonderful to light your fire!

Another of my challenging prints has two rectangles on one side, the rest plain white. This can't be turned in any odd direction because the design is a very elaborate pavillion – a tent.

It would have to be used right-side-up only. This one just may end up being a jacket lining and not a garment to be seen at all.

It's no wonder some of these remain in my collection for long periods of time – maybe forever without being used. The decision of how to use it can be very difficult. I suspect I buy some of these things out of curiosity, wondering what they can become, a real challenge. I buy it to find out as I wait for that piece to speak to me. They can remain strangely silent for an interminable time. Just remember with any of these that being a sewer means you are in control and can tame even the wildest print. Lots of luck!

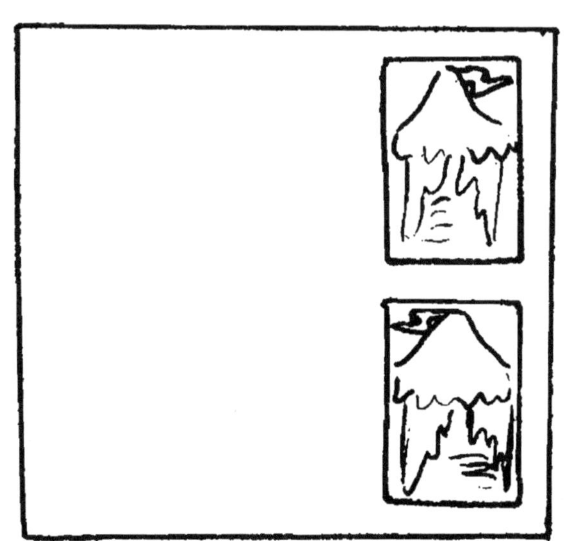

One of the lovely things about making your own clothing and working with fabrics is that you have such incredible freedom. You can find such perfect color matches unavailable to those who have to buy their clothing. If you can't find it, you can create it.

For example, maybe I want to wear an olive blouse with purple pants. Some might think that a strange combination unless another article is worn with them which has that color combination. It could be a scarf whose print carries both colors. It could be a belt I have with that color combination in leather. A jacket or a vest with both those colors would make it even more obvious. It is quite easy to create such a garment which will tie the two together even if you have to partially create the fabric.

A handwoven fabric recently purchased is very interesting in its yarn combinations. At one selvage the warp yarns are more plum and they gradually progress to something closer to burgundy by the time you get over to the other selvage. In between the two edges are several hints of greens and blue greens. Purple is the overall impression. That can be changed.

A wonderful yarn I found is of two strands very loosely twisted. The mohair one is variegated from purple to olive. The metallic and silk strand is more strongly in the gold-greens. Hand woven fabrics are usually loose enough to weave more yarn into them and that's exactly what I did. Using a tapestry needle (quite large with blunt point and big eye) this weaving on your lap is a great way to watch television on a chilly evening. The fabric was like being wrapped in and warmed by a throw. The yarns are only woven in here and there, but really make a difference.

Next I backed the whole piece of fabric with a new HTC fusible interfacing called Textured Weft. Perfect for this use, it holds all those potentially ravelly fabric yarns in place yet it stays absolutely soft with a sweatery quality like no other interfacing. The fabric can now be cut without being in danger of falling apart.

It wasn't a large piece of fabric and unfortunately would only fit the bodice back and front of a jacket pattern, no room for sleeves. A vest? Logical, but I'm holding out for a jacket At my favorite local shop I found a plum wool crepe that was a great blend. I bought enough for pants, a long sleeved blouse, and the extra sleeves for the jacket.

By the way, support those local fabric shops in your area. I hear all of us moaning when another independent fabric shop closes its door. Please remember that to keep those doors open. *We* have to keep walking in, and buying those things we love, we need, we deserve. All those fabric shops depend on us to buy, just as we need them to furnish our necessities. This partnership deserves nurturing and maintaining.

I also found in the shop the perfect button. Its interior looks like woven yarns in the same colors. It never ceases to amaze me how the most exquisitely wonderful thing, just right for the project, is available if you look.

The solid wool sleeves needed to have something to more closely tie to the front and back. The obvious is more of that same purple-chartreuse yarn. This fabric is quite closely woven however, and the textury yarn can't realistically be woven into it. The alternative is applying it to the surface. This is what you see in the photo section. That sleeve isn't covered in straight lines as the cover jacket is. Remember all the back and forth stitching that looked like ripples in water in chapter 5? I used that same design here but this time it was stitching invisibly with clear monofilament thread and it was anchoring that yarn onto the sleeve. The device for this miracle to take place is of course, my beloved New Home Miracle Stitcher. This gadget holds the yarn up close to the needle and you can stitch in any direction while applying it. ***NEWS FLASH!!!*** Now available in New Home shops, is a new model of the Miracle Stitcher that has a short shank to fit other than the MemoryCraft 9000 and 8000 models. Check to see if it will work on your machine. It only took a few minutes to embellish each sleeve, fabric in a **51** round hoop. Holding the hoop spring handles in one hand, anyone can do a really nice job with this stitching quickly, moving the hoop a little slower back and forth.

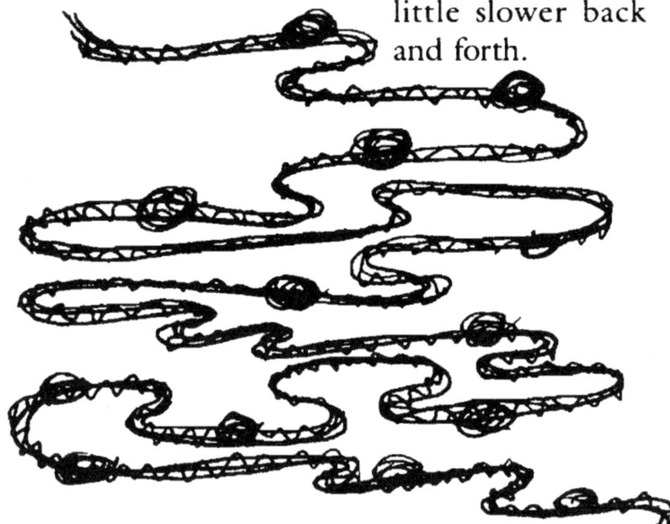

This yarn was one of the most difficult yarns I've used with the Miracle Stitcher because of its double strand, the two wanting to go separate directions. They were mostly just parallel, barely twisted at all. Any problem can be overcome and the answer here is just stopping periodically, wetting my finger and twisting the strand by rolling it between thumb and finger, then stitching on.

Two ways can so far change the color of fabric, weaving into it and embellishing on top of it. Other fabrics suggest other alternatives. Last series there was a program on mesh fabrics and these have endless opportunities for change. They ravel easily which means fringing is a distinct possibility. If they ravel on the edge, how about in the interior? Because of the very open weave yarns can be pulled out to make a design

by the airy path resulting. Back to weaving, think of all the pretties which could be woven into these open spaces. In a piece of charcoal mesh it didn't matter what I wove in – it all looked terrific.

One thought is silk embroidery ribbon. Those narrow little strips in multi colors looked very pretty as the charcoal took on a very festive mood. An organdy ribbon about $\frac{3}{8}$" wide looked magnificent as it was pulled through. The ribbon is variegated in several tints and shades of grays and browns and displays a more sophisticated look. This meant several yarns needed to be pulled out of the same space to produce a wide enough channel. I used a tapestry needle for this and it worked very well, but a bodkin or one with a clamp to hold the ribbon firmly might be your best answer. These needn't be woven over, under, every yarn as it just doesn't show easily how expertly your work is done. If what you pull through is quite smooth, you might try tying it on (same as you do with serger thread on your serger). This is just terrific to not even bother weaving, just pulling, but won't necessarily work on all fabrics. It usually is impossible to advocate some technique as *the* way. There are too many variables.

In that charcoal mesh it mattered little what I tried. Cords, yarns, everything looked marvelous. Some fabrics simply lend themselves to any additions, deletions as is your whim.

The fabric I used on the beginning project, the sleeves of the jacket and the matching slacks, was still going strong. Enough for another project, it is a long sleeve blouse which zips in back and has a high jewel neck in front. Its sleeves are unique in that they open down the center and the space is filled by a bias cut tube of self-

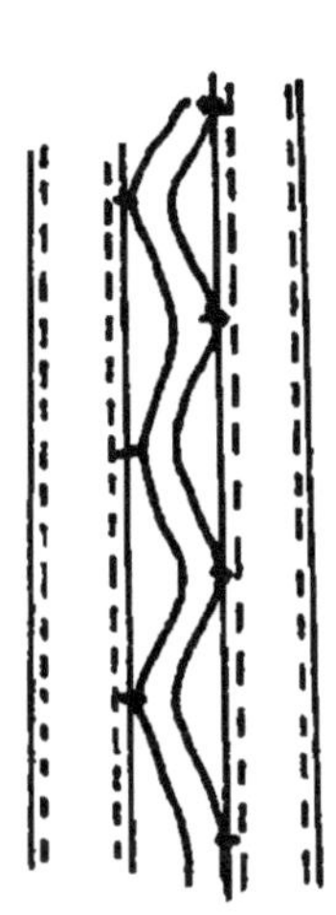

fabric turned right side out with a Fasturn. This was thoroughly explained in a program of tubes in series 16 so I won't expand on that feature now. Here the story is the ribbons which are variegated purple to olive also. They border each side of the sleeve tube on the sleeve, topstitched a reach edge. The blouse front then has a whole series of these sewn on with graduated spacing as they are close together at the top, spreading farther apart as they progress lower.

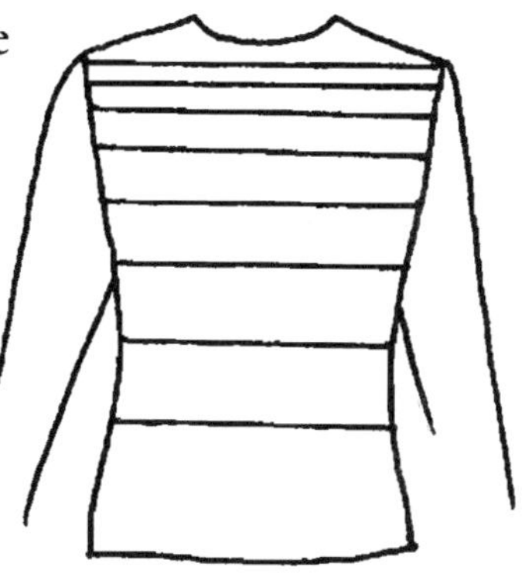

Five to ten years ago all these wonderful trims weren't widely available. Maybe I've just become more aware of them recently or maybe, because we all enjoy embellishing more than we use to, they actually are more plentiful in shops everywhere. Even in the most mundane chain fabric shop today, an enormous variety of lovely organdy ribbons in every color and width can be found.

The rhubarb vest and pants in another center book photo are embellished to promote a color change or at least a color coordination. We've become so much more broad minded in putting colors together and liking odd mixtures. I suppose this is comparable to the way food tastes have changed through the years. I remember when wearing pink and red together was absolutely taboo but that combination became respectable many years ago and we keep moving on. I decided to put that rhubarb outfit with a deep purple blouse because something about it just appealed to me. Here also yarn was the answer and the inspiration behind the mixture.

This yarn is a blend of dull reds into a touch of chartreuse and purples. Again, it is couched liberally on the vest front.

This was just an ordinary vest pattern. What makes it different is the addition of the band at the front and neck. The band is a straight strip of fabric and to stitch it on creates a stand-up collar. The band is the exact length of the vest neckline plus end seams, cut **4"** wide. Interface, fold in half wrong side out and stitch ends. Turn right side out and press. Attach to vest neckline. If your neckline tends to gap because of a prominent bust, use this band to ease in the bias area on each side between the arrows.

This is an obvious place for yarn stripes, with row upon row of them striping the fabric. It was difficult to stop when I liked the effect better and better the more I added. They soon spilled off the collar and fanned out down the vest right front. All these straight lines are couched on with monofilament thread so the stitching doesn't even show.

Any kind of a foot that holds the yarn in place while you stitch over it will do the job. This includes several possibilities and I like to have every foot New Home has because each specific foot allows you to do a new process you can't do without it. These accessory pieces can make the job so easy. As each of my rows fanned out wider at the bottom I then again went to the Miracle Stitcher to fill the spaces. It allows the freedom of going in spirals rather than just straight forward.

One side only is usually my preference in doing these things, or at least going more heavily on the one side than the other. Something about this asymmetrical balance I really like. It's very rare that I would balance the two sides equally.

Some of the new threads change color for some added fun. In the Coats and Clark award winning new Twist group, their color combinations twisted together make for marvelous blending if you are interested in "thread painting" pictures from nature. Flowers, leaves, birds, etc., can be fabulous done with Twist using free motion stitching. You will use an embroidery foot and drop feed dogs. I love C &C's new stripe threads that change color at regular intervals. Notice the black vest in the photo pages with it irregularly spaced multi-color stripes. To do this, select one of the stripe threads. Draw a series of stripes across the interfaced vest fronts with a chalk wheel or other fabric marker and a yardstick. Set your machine on its widest satin stitch. Spend some very relaxing time while your mind wanders anywhere it pleases as you stitch away, following those lines. The colors change about every $\frac{1}{2}$".

www.makeitcoats.com

In my fabric collection I found the cotton print for a lining which echoes all the thread colors. In my button collection I found an incredible match. A square button composed of 9 little squares in the same colors as the thread looked like it was all made for each other.

Neutral Accents Chapter 12

I saw a wonderful fabric in a shop. It is a burnished metallic giving it an antique look. Depending on how the light hits its tiny pleats, it looks a little between the colors of pewter and purple. Intriguing as its appearance is, it feels harsh. I wouldn't want a whole garment of it

The fiber content is silk in the main part with a lot of metallic yarns. If you would make a whole garment, it might be a dressy top or a slim tubular shaped skirt. Or buy a small quantity of it to use as an accent fabric. Dream up spectacular uses for it and even if on the pricey side, it will pay its way.

The vest worn on this program is a remnant left over from a pair of slacks. In a very somber dark taupe, it doesn't generate very much excitement near the face. This is just asking for some embellishment and an idea takes place. Let's keep it colorless, just using the accent fabric in this crinkly pleated texture.

Because of its metallic content, good additions would be an assortment of metallic threads and fine cords. Again almost devoid of noticeable color, I chose a selection in raisin, pinky-brown, dull pewter and any others that would blend in but give a little subdued glitter and glamour. I began this selection process in my usual way as I always feel one of the best parts of sewing is at this beginning stage when everything comes together and the raw materials are assembled.

On my table is the fabric that will be used, as it will be the backdrop for all the embellishment to follow. All the possible extras are placed around it to see what wants to go together, what should be eliminated. From drawers and cabinets I pull all sorts of buttons, cords, braids, threads, beads and in this case, that accent fabric. By the time I eliminated the ho-hum choices, the components that remained were perfect together.

There are several ways these threads and cords might be applied after first cutting out the fabric and fusing interfacing to its backside. The most obvious is to just sew on with an

elongated (3.5-4.) straight stitch if the thread is fine enough to thread through a needle. A topstitching or embroidery needle with a bigger eye might do the job.

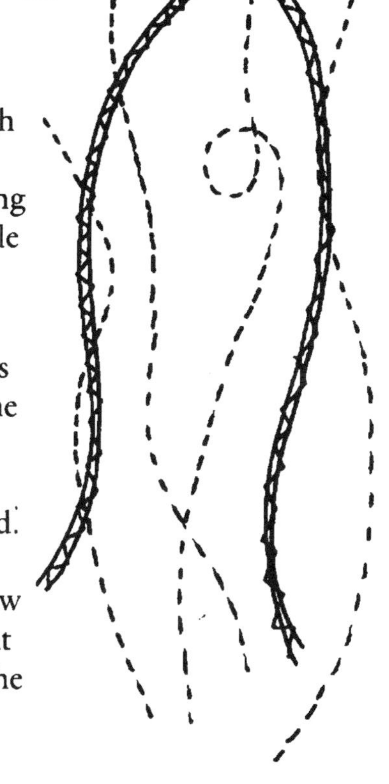

Another cord is large enough that the only possibility is couching it on with monofilament thread. Make these stitches fairly long but narrow enough in width that they blend in with the cord, remaining invisible.

The rest were suitable to wind on bobbins and stitch on the fabric – wrong side up. This intermediate group is too large to thread a needle but too small to bother couching on. This needn't be done by hand. Simply wind the bobbin in the usual manner. You will probably need to wind several bobbins because the sizes of the thread/cord fill the spaces on the bobbin quickly. Again, use large stitches. What thread is used through the needle doesn't matter since it will appear on the interfacing side.

Treat that bobbin-wound cord like any thread if it is small enough, pulling it through the bobbin tension spring. If you find pulling it by hand that it doesn't move because it is too large, by-pass the tension spring, and pull it up through the throat plate hole. Going like this directly from bobbin through the hole, the stitches will be a little loopy, but since this is a textured piece, the stitch quality will make it that much more interesting.

When we travel on business I never take my sewing machine. The van is already overloaded with more than 100 garments, two big clothes racks, seminar sample boxes, and hundreds of books and videos for live seminars.

What I do take is handwork too time-consuming to do in my sewing room. On the road as John drives, I'm the passenger with hours between stops. I can accomplish many things, finishing up projects began at home.

On this trip I took that partially completed vest and a gallon zip lock plastic bag of accent fabric, pin cushion, scissors, needle and thread, copper colored glass bugle beads. What I did not have was the slightest notion of what I was going to do with it all. No matter. One has only to look around to find a good idea in a matter of minutes.

At a stoplight up the road we halted in front of a flower shop. The obvious hit me. Flowers, of course! No need for realism, imaginary flowers would do just fine. Mine would be sort of like morning glories on a vine.

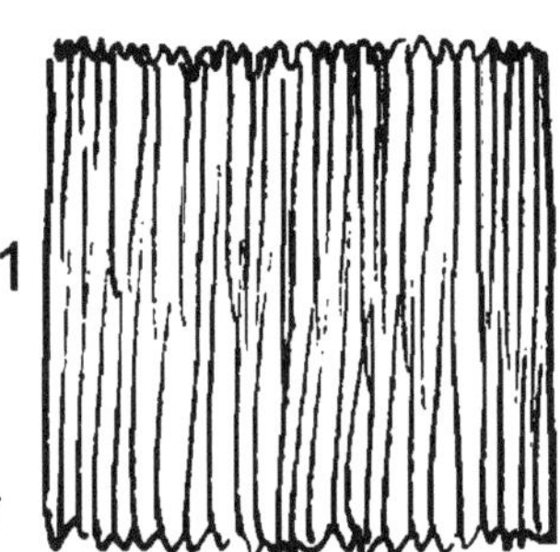

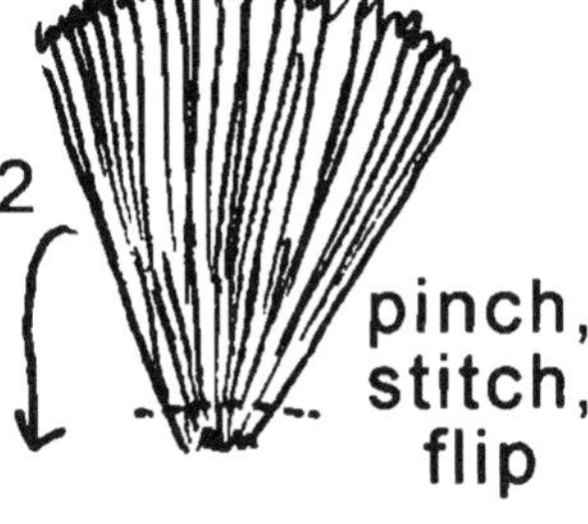

From my crinkly fabric I cut a square about 2" on all sides. One end of this I pinched together, the other end I fanned out wider. Turn under all raw edges and stitch down all around with little hand stitches. A few bugle beads for accent and it sparkled beautifully. Elegantly subdued but just an eye-catching glint to warrant a second look. What fun this was. It took a lot of time, but it was a very profitable way to fill the time between Indiana and Florida. Later at home as I finished the vest I used more of this accent fabric to pipe all edges for a finished look.

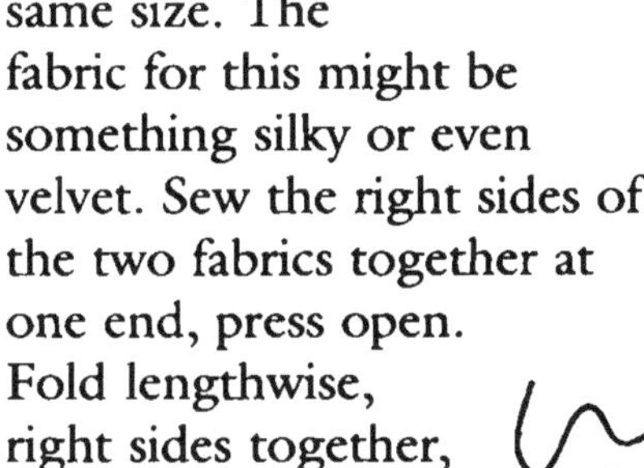

On a day between seminars in Florida I shopped in a multitude of little specialty shops – the pricey resort variety. I was so tickled to see that identical fabric used in many ways. Here are some of them following.

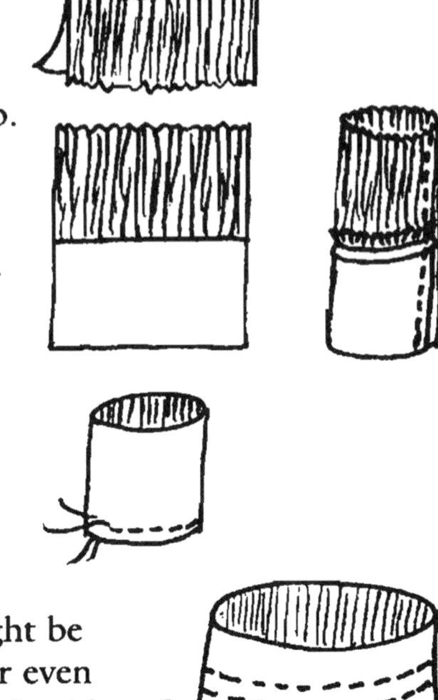

A little evening pouch ($65) was just lovely in one shop. To make, begin with a crinkled fabric 14^W x 10^L. This is the size of the fabric when relaxed, as it can be stretched out to at least twice this size. Cut a lining fabric the same size. The fabric for this might be something silky or even velvet. Sew the right sides of the two fabrics together at one end, press open. Fold lengthwise, right sides together, and sew another seam. Press. Now peel the lining down over the outside fabric so the raw edges are together. At the fold edge crease and carefully press. Run a gathering stitch around the raw lower edges through both fabrics together. About $1\frac{1}{2}$" from the top fold stitch two lines of stitching to form a casing. Draw up the lower gathering, stitch snugly and tie all thread ends tightly. The lining side of the fabric will have a raw edge at the gathering. Cut a little circle of fabric, maybe 2" in diameter.

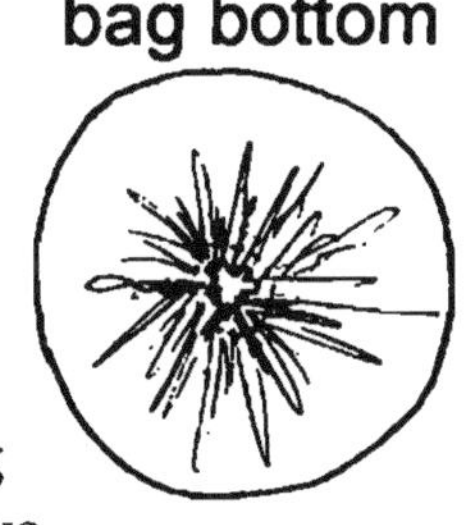

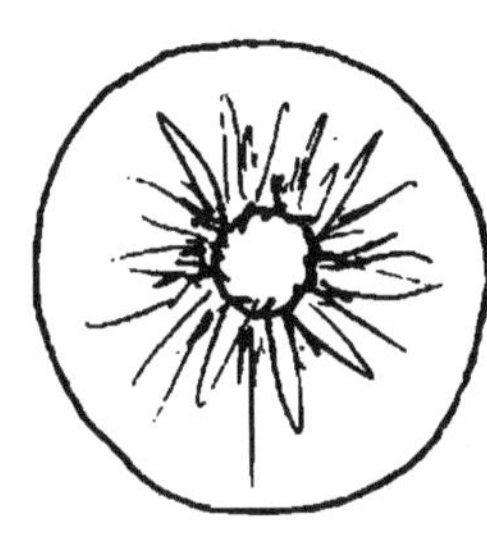

Turn under its edges and stitch down by hand to finish.

Turn the bag right side out. On each side of the bag cut two little slits about 1" apart, outer fabric only. If this is a crinkly fabric they won't show, and the fabric won't fray. If your fabric is smooth, plan in advance and way back at the outset stitch little eyelets or button holes instead. With a safety pin or bodkin pull a cord through one opening all around the whole casing, and out the other opening next to it. Do the same with a second cord or ribbon from the opposite bag side. This way when you pull the two cords the bag gathers close. Open it with your fingers through the top ruffle. Attach beads to cord or ribbon ends for a completed look and maybe some other beads would be pretty on the bag's surface.

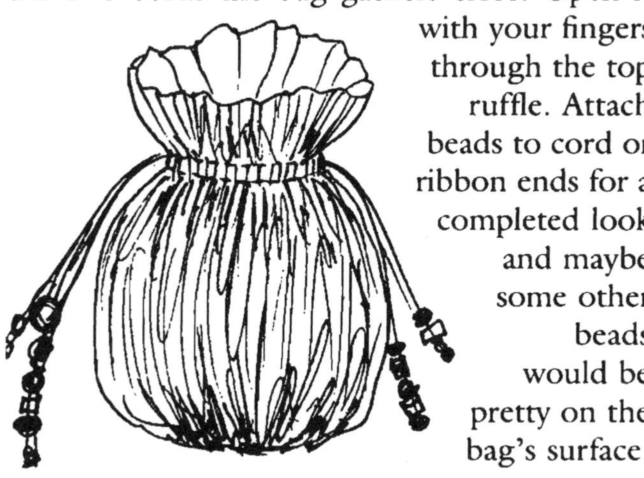

I gave it a posh look with ribbon flowers. Other dressy fabrics could be used instead of ribbon. In which case, cut on the bias. Fold the fabric strip in half lengthwise. Begin at one end and stitch a curve from the fold down to the doubled raw edges, along its length, and curve back up to the fold at the other end. Trim off excess at corners. Draw up this gathering stitch somewhat. Begin to roll one end making a few hand stitches to

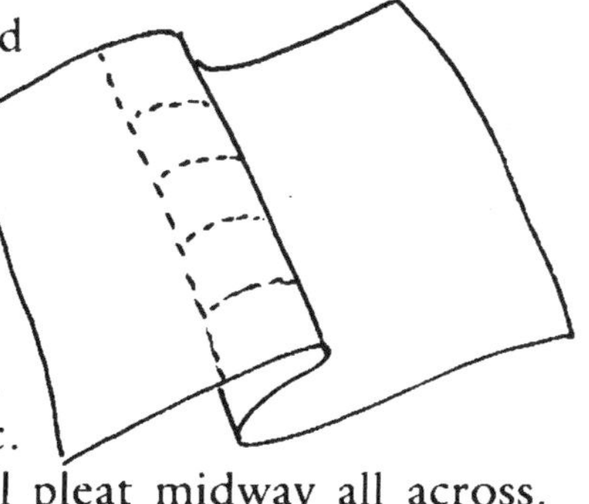

hold as you keep rolling. Secure everything at the raw gathered edge flower bottom. Now "peel" the flower inside out so the raw edges are all concealed within and it looks finished from every angle. Stitch several of these on the bag for a charming little formal purse.

If you would like to make this a travel jewelry bag, way back at the beginning cut the lining fabric 4" or 5" longer than the outside fabric. Stitch a horizontal pleat midway all across. Smooth the pleat upward and stitch a series of lines making little compartments for sets of earrings, etc. Complete the bag as before.

Using the same crinkled fabric, here are some other little projects you might want to make. A vest clip would be just the right finish to shape in a back waist effectively. A set of these two clip ends needed are found on a card in the button section of a fabric shop. The saw-tooth-edged clamps anchor onto the vest parts for wearing. To make, cut a piece of elastic the width of the clip opening in the length you want – probably 8" or 9". Stitch a tube of decorative fabric the correct size to fit over elastic.

Remember the elastic stretches out, so this decorative fabric should be cut longer and crush on the elastic when not extended. Turn the tube right side out and pull the elastic through its interior with a bodkin or large safety pin. With fabric extending about $\frac{3}{8}$" beyond the elastic ends the raw edges can later be turned under for a neat finish. Somewhere near the elastic ends, machine stitch through layers to hold elastic and fabric tube together. Insert these ends through the clip loops and secure with hand stitches on the wrong side. On the right side I put more ribbon

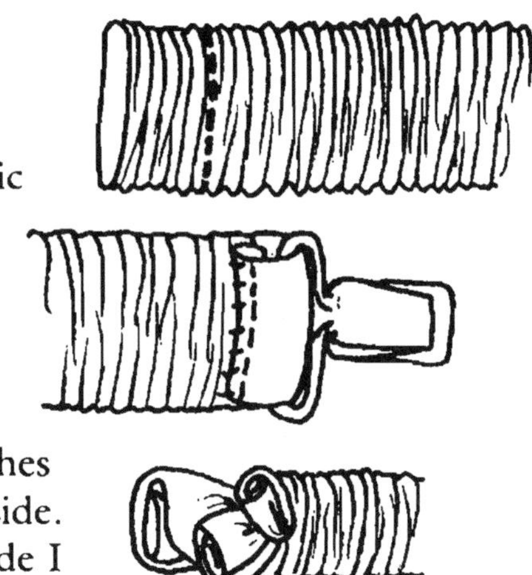

flowers at each end to conceal the clips. The cost was near $30 in the shop where I saw it – mine less than $2.

Need hostess gifts? How about pretty little gifts for yourself to keep your spirits soaring? Sachets for drawers or closets or just on surfaces in a bedroom are nice. These are just little square

bags, maybe 3" each direction when finished. Initially cut larger at whichever side will be left open for stuffing. Fill with all potpourri or a combination of that and fiberfill. Whip the opening closed by hand and in doing one end, I enclosed the end of a wide velvet ribbon. The finish is more fabric flowers clustered at the ribbon base, the loose end cut in a V. Several of these are virtually free rather than the commercial $$$ in the teen range. If giving, cluster several on package wrap along with, or instead of, a bow.

Pretty pillows come from a small amount of accent fabric. One side a complimentary fabric, the back another choice. If the fabric of choice is limited

in quantity combine with others and do something in patchwork. This blends well with a combination of fashion and upholstery fabrics, whatever you have in a nice blend of colors and textures.

One of my favorite ideas for this I saw in a magazine. The price wasn't given, but because of the designer's familiar name, I knew that jacket cost several thousand dollars. To my delight, a fabric similar to my accent fabric was used with lots of stitching to create a design on the surface, while quilting it to a backing. This stitched design surrounding plain areas rather resembles a flagstone terrace. I can think of two ways to duplicate the look. One is to do the stitching wrong side up. Not enough fabric for a jacket, I did this as a formal clutch bag. Start by cutting the basic shape in fusible fleece which will be suitably firm for this purse project. For a jacket I would use sew-in, not fusible. The pattern is of course, my Clutch Bag pattern available from our office. Position this

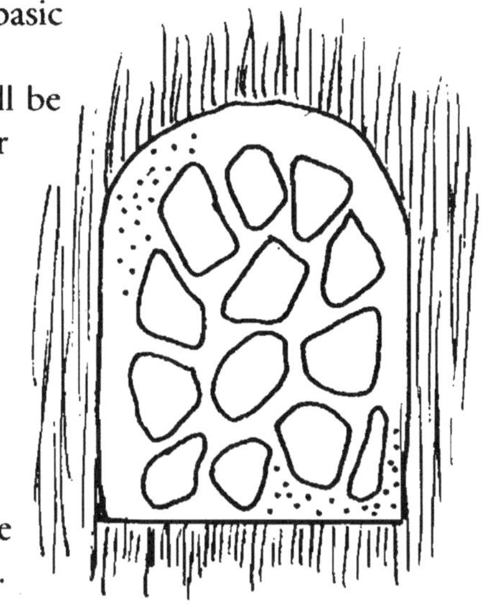

fusible form, fusible side down, over the fabric, wrong side up. Fuse, then trim away the excess fabric. I used a disappearing marker to draw a design that resembled the magazine photo. With metallic cord wound on the bobbin, any thread on top, drop the feed dog so you can control the direction you stitch. Use an embroidery foot and set the machine on straight stitch. The fusible fleece is so firm, no embroidery hoop is

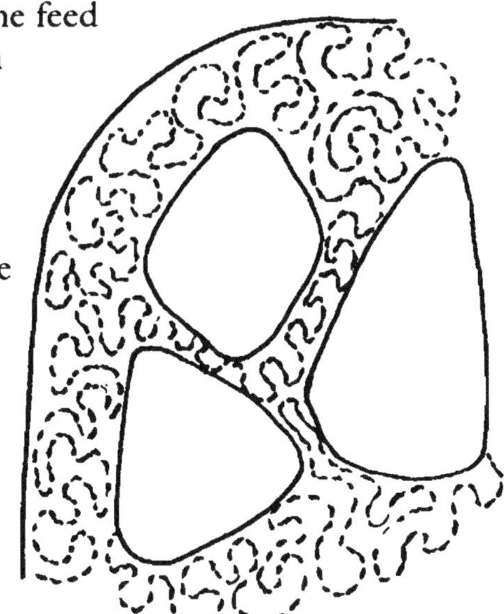

needed to hold it taut. Move the fabric around slowly but stitch rather fast and fill all the area surrounding the flagstones or whatever design you want to create. Within a few minutes the whole thing is stitched and you can proceed with construction of the project.

If your cord is too thick for bobbin work the perfect answer is New Home's Miracle Stitcher. Even if you don't have my Memorycraft 9000 with its long shank, this now comes in a short shank version that may fit your machine, whatever the brand. Check with your local New Home/Janome dealer to see if it works on your machine. I've described its workings many times before but basically it's a foot that allows you to couch heavier cord, yarns, ribbons, in any direction working right side up. Drop the feed dog, use monofilament thread on top, any bobbin thread. The Miracle Stitch foot will hold the cord up close to the needle, zigzagging it down while you move the fabric around. This is a thoroughly delightful addition to your equipment I heartily recommend. It does some processes nothing else can do.

The next time you see an irresistible fabric you really love but can't envision a whole garment of it, consider buying a small amount to use as an accent fabric or for similar small projects. These pretty things are food for the soul – life enrichers!

At the start of this series I said *color* is the big turn-on when it comes to fabric selection. You all have some favorites that you can't resist. When I saw this particular fabric, however, I was attracted by the fact that every color I could possibly wear was in it, or at least every bright jewel color. Not for the faint-of-heart, there were no pastels, nothing held back or subdued. This raw silk beautifully takes on brilliantly hued dyes, and the maker used them all.

I could imagine it going over that deep cherry red skirt or the lipstick red pants as a few different red varieties were represented. Ditto for many intense blues, greens, purples. It would simply go with about everything I have, and a jacket would therefore be the obvious garment to make of it.

Some silks are lovely to feel, soft, luxuriously tender, and you can't keep your hands away. Not this fabric. It was quite coarse, the yarns fat and wiry. To make matters worse, it felt rather grimy despite the clarity of colors, as though gritty clay had been rubbed into it. I bought it anyway because color is a mighty dictator.

My work was cut out for me with a trip to the dry cleaner the obvious starting point. Any fabric whose fat yarns ravel this easily, almost falling off the cut ends without even being touched, better first be secured. A serger finish is the usual way but even that would not deter this fraying. The yarn would still fall off, serger edging attached. About three rows of slightly overlapping wide machine zigzag stitches proved to be a very successful deterrent and held edges in place. It came back from the cleaners not only feeling clean and free from grit, but considerably softer.

In this type fabric, fraying will always be a problem. Fusing a backing to it is a necessity. Experience the new interfacings and backings as they appear on the market. One fairly new one that I love for this particular problem is Textured Weft from HTC. It is very soft so doesn't stiffen the fashion fabric at all. It merely holds everything together perfectly. Before Textured Weft, I would have used So Sheer, Sof Brush, or maybe (slightly heavier) Fusi Knit. Depending of the individual set of circumstances, I might fuse the whole length of fabric with this Textured Weft for the backing. I might cut out the individual pattern pieces in the interfacing, later fusing each to the back side of the fashion fabric. The former saves a little fabric. The latter saves a little more time, but might be more difficult space wise. Your ironing board is of a limited size, and doesn't provide a lot of space for this process. Consider HTC Space Boards: the large one folds in half for storage, but opened up is 51^W x 33^L and is wonderful on my cutting table making an easy job of this. It is a padded board with a grid printed on the cotton drill cover.

Because of the fabric problems, it is smart to choose a pattern with no fussy details. With the multi-colors and fat textured yarns, nothing detailed would show as it would in a hard-finished fabric. Keep it simple with as few seams as possible. Because it's rather thick, pare it down and eliminate unnecessary bulk. The pattern being used here has a center back seam, but no shape in it. Since it is perfectly straight it is sensible to overlap. Cut this on a center back fold in a one-piece back. If it were a thin, sleek, clear-faced fabric I might keep the seam and top-stitch it in a welt to emphasize and add vertical emphasis. When combining pieces be sure to position the pattern stitching line (NOT the cutting line) on the fabric fold.

This pattern also had a two-piece sleeve, a back and front with a seam down the center. This also would be quite attractive in a smooth clear-faced fabric or leather, both as a design feature, and also as a means of eliminating too much

fullness in the sleeve cap which will not ease in because of the firm fabric quality. Not a problem with this loosely woven fabric as you could ease in a considerable amount, but since it doesn't show it's sensible to make it a one-piece sleeve and treat the top gap as a dart.

That sleeve is a good feature to file away in your mind for future use. It allows more space in the biceps area if you need it there but tapers to a slimmer wrist where width is not needed. I consider every commercial pattern a learning tool when you see a good idea. If you can take a two-piece sleeve and combine them to make one piece, the reverse is also possible. You could easily split a one-piece sleeve pattern to accomplish two things: add width in the biceps while eliminating a wedge at the top center to get rid of too much fullness. Life is a constant learning process and little revelations hit you everyday which add to your knowledge, your level of expertise.

If that overlap is good in loosely woven fabric on a two-piece sleeve, wouldn't it also be good to eliminate a front edge seam and cut the bodice front and facing as one? Then the front edge would be just a smooth flat fold as the facing turns inside rather than a potentially ravelly, bulky seam. This works if the fabric is wide enough to accommodate that bigger piece

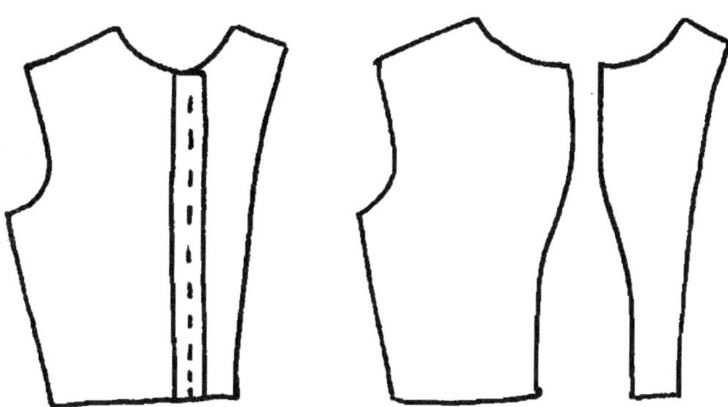

and also it works when this front edge is a completely straight line. If this pattern has shaped, flaring lapel edges it will not work. The facing must be cut separately unless you change the styling.

Another choice on the neck and front facings would be to have no regulation enclosed seams. You could instead lay wrong sides together and staystitch. Then bind the raw edges with a complimentary fabric for a bold accent. Bias cut of this is a woven fabric, cut crosswise if it is a knit, synthetic suede or leather.

Because there are so many colors in this fabric you have to make a decision on which to go with for the button color. I decided on a deep red set into a brass decorative framework. This limits it to wearing gold jewelry whereas I usually wear silver, but the colors over all seemed to point to gold. If you don't want to commit but would rather change buttons to go with a variety of coordinating garments, consider making eyelets instead of sewing them on. This could be attached from the backside by those little clips found on shanked button cards. Save a bunch of these to have on hand when needed.

Because of the extreme raveling problem, even though the fabric is held together by fusible interfacing I decided to go with buttonloops. In this case they were just made by twisting long yarns from the fabric to the extreme (by hand or on the machine bobbin winder). When they are twisted very tightly, they will backwind from the center producing a thick 4-ply cord. This machine zigzagged down the jacket right front edge leaving open places wherever a buttonloop 61 is needed. Backstitch or lock stitch at each loop end. The textured fabric hides the stitches and they can't be seen at all.

You may have noticed I've used this same simple jacket pattern several times in this series including the book cover. The reason is, it is such a simple, shapeless jacket and my main emphasis has been in embellishment or in using unusual fabrics. When the focus is on either of these, simple styling works best.

This simple jacket would be terrific as a blouse, too. The thin blue crepe overblouse and pant outfit I made to wear under this jacket is a case in point. To use a jacket pattern to make a blouse, a few changes are in order. Do you want the shoulder pads that were allowed in the jacket pattern? Will they be the same size? If flatter changes are made here, slope the shoulder seams downward out toward the armscye to eliminate some height so the bodice will hang smoothly. To neglect doing so will result in diagonal wrinkles when worn. It is also likely that converting jacket to blouse, the shoulders need to be narrowed since other garments won't be worn under this blouse. Usually it involves $\frac{1}{2}$" at the shoulder point tapering off to nothing where the armscye notch is.

That sleeve can be changed in several ways. In the thinner blouse fabric without lining it would be quite loose. You could leave it as is but at the wrist flatten it and sew a buttonhole after hemming it. This would then fold over sideways to button into a slim wrist. Another way would be to overlap the pattern pieces at the center to simply make a narrow sleeve. Remember you have to keep the elbow area wide enough to allow comfortable arm bending.

I decided this would be an overblouse, but didn't want it to just hang loose. A waistline casing and drawstring belt would give it definition, personality. Try it on to see where the waistline is and mark it. I want this to blouse a little so I would put the casing (bias tape made from a lining fabric) about 1" below the actual waistline. Previous to this I had also cut extra flare and length to make an attractive peplum effect below the belt.

Reinforce the points where the casing will end on the blouse inside. Fuse a 2" circle of thin interfacing here. On the outside, through the reinforced blouse layer, construct a machine buttonhole. The size is the width of the casing. Then sew the casing bias tape in place. Its ends will cover the buttonholes just made. The casing will be stitched down outside the buttonhole stitching so that the opening for the belt leads to the outside.

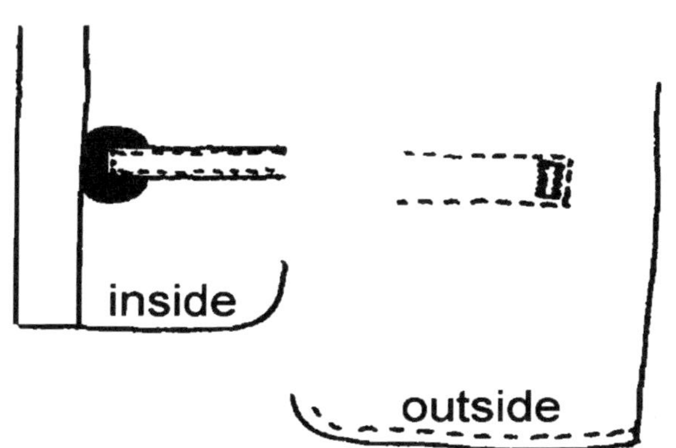

The belt is cut on the bias for a softer drape, stitched and turned over a Fasturn, but strung through with a cable cord for stability. It is about 15" longer than the garment circumference. Gathered up it produces a soft droopy bow. Brass tips found in the notions department 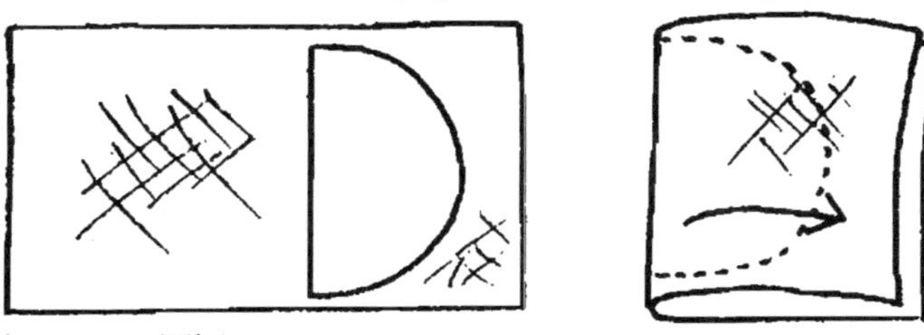 are fabric glued on the ends for a commercial look.

Shoulder pads in such unlined garments can be removable, especially if the garment will be washed. If dry cleaned I like to permanently sew them in to help preserve the shape on a  hanger. Thin commercial pads can be easily covered by cutting a bias piece of lining fabric (or any comfortable silky fabric) slightly more than twice the pad size. Fold it over enclosing 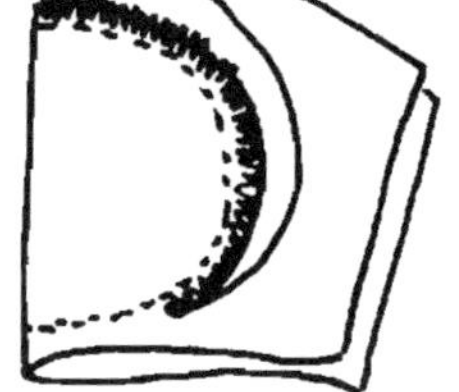

the pad within layers. Pin all around slightly catching the pad edge. Machine stitch on the pin line, removing as you come up to them. Serge outside the stitching line to finish edge while cutting off excess.

I could make a whole wardrobe of this one pattern – or any pattern by changing the styling slightly each time. It would never be recognized by the time you vary all components plus the fabrics and embellishments. The beauty of this repetition is that you know how it fits and once altered, you never have to change it again.

Consider all those shoppers who have to take in ready-to-wear only what is available to them in shops. Aren't you glad you sew and can create anything you want? What enormous freedom you have and to realize that *YES, you really can do this!*

I seem to be finishing program #221 of The Sewing Connection the same way I began program #1, and every other program along the way. I'm making decisions, making changes, thinking through the best way to do anything for top quality results because quality is the only way to go.

We've based every show in this series 17 on a color and this Coat of Many Colors is the last of the lineup. So, what color is my world? It is an absolute rainbow of happy hues. Life is lovely if you choose to do your favorite things, and sewing is at the top of my list.

Viewers have frequently asked won't I ever run out of ideas? The answer is no, I never would. If it were program 5,000 I would still have endless exciting directions to take sewing. Look around you - there are no bounds.

This though, is more than the end of series 17. It is also the end of an era. It's the last Sewing Connection Series program because other options, other colors are beckoning and I need time to pursue them. Many of my programs will still be seen on public television and if you missed any, they're all available from our office in video and book form. Your continued support of public television through your calls, letters, and pledges will keep Sewing Connection series programs repeating, and keep other sewing programs alive and well and on the air, too.

I want to thank everyone involved with this whole production: my family, people in our office and in the production studio. Certainly thanks to the program underwriters whose products I believe in, and use constantly in my own sewing room as well as in the studio. The right equipment certainly makes the job simple and pleasurable.

Then I really want to thank all of you, the viewers. Through the years I've had thousands of cards and letters, expressions of friendship, and I feel a genuine affection for you all. Sewers are the nicest people and I want to stay connected since that's the whole premise of this show. I'm Shirley Adams and from The Sewing Connection - now and always - I wish you joy.

These are some of the people who over the years have made The Sewing Connection possible – and fun. Larson Productions and all the members of their staff are like family. Missing are Kathy, Debbie and Kate, only because I am not a professional photographer and they can run very fast.

Made in the USA
Monee, IL
07 July 2026

56553280R00040